A MYSTERIOUS SPIRIT
THE BELL WITCH
OF TENNESSEE

By
CHARLES BAILEY BELL
(A Descendant)

HARRIET PARKS MILLER

FACSIMILE REPRODUCTION 1972
BY
CHARLES ELDER—BOOKSELLER
PUBLISHER
NASHVILLE, TENNESSEE

THE BELL WITCH

A Mysterious Spirit

By

CHARLES BAILEY BELL, M.D.

For some years Instructor on the Brain and Nervous System at Medical Department of the University of Nashville, for several years on Visiting Staff of Nashville City Hospital. Was Member of Tennessee State Medical Association, Nashville Academy of Medicine and other medical organizations, etc., etc.

Copyright, 1934, By
CHARLES BAILEY BELL

CONTENTS

I. A Biographical Sketch of Members of the Bell Family.

II. The Spirit Makes Its Appearance at the Bell Home.

III. Recollections Given by Some of the Slaves.

IV. The Spirit's Kindness and High Regard for Mrs. John Bell.

V. Betsy Bell's Trying Experiences with the Spirit.

VI. Recollections of Richard Williams Bell.

VII. John Bell Jr.'s, Recollections of the Spirit.

VIII. John Bell Jr.'s, Recollections of the Spirit On Its Return Visit.

IX. Recollections of Dr. Joel Thomas Bell.

PREFACE

For many years articles have appeared in many magazines and newspapers giving sensational stories regarding the so-called Bell Witch (?). During the last year or two these articles have appeared very frequently. I presume the cause for the more frequent articles, some in serial form, has been that it was the time claimed for another promised visit from the Witch (?). Such articles have even appeared in European papers, so I have been told.

The Author so many times has had inquiries from different parts of the country, from New York to the western coast, asking his opinion of the Witch, that he knows thousands of people are very much interested at this time in getting the best information obtainable regarding one of the greatest mysteries the world has ever known.

Wherever he has been, from California to the East coast, down in Mexico, in the South, or North, he has been asked if he were one of the Bells of the "Bell Witch" family. In answer to all these inquiries he has followed the actions of his ancestors and not given any information worth while. The members of the Bell family have talked very little even to their own families, and practically not at all to strangers or friends regarding this mystery.

The name "Bell Witch" has always been resented by the family. They are sensitive to such an appellation. The "Bell Witch" was not the old woman kind that was known so well in the East and Europe many years ago, and in many instances burned at the stake. Neither was it the kind that could be punished in any way; with all its tangible actions it had the faculty of vanishing instantly.

The Author shall relate in this book what was handed down to him by his father, Dr. J. T. Bell, he having the recollections of his father, John Bell Jr.

Joel Thomas Bell was the oldest son of John Bell Jr. He was born April 13, 1831, in Robertson County, and died March 30, 1910. He resembled his father very much, being a man of striking appearance, six feet two inches tall, broad-shouldered and of an extraordinarily intellectual appearance.

After a good literary education, he studied medicine, entering the Medical Department of the University of Nashville in 1853, and graduating from that institution after the usual course of lectures then required. He began the practice of medicine at his home, his father's house, within a few hundred yards of the old home site of his grandfather, John Bell.

He married Laura Virginia Henry, daughter of Captain Lemuel Henry of Robertson County. His home was built on land given him by his father. (The farm now belongs to the Author.) He practiced medicine fifty years at Adams. He established an extensive practice and was highly regarded as a diagnostician by every doctor who asked for his services in consultation.

Many people now living in Robertson County and adjoining counties remember him with genuine pleasure. He followed the rule of the older Bells—if he told anything at all it was always the truth. No one who knew him ever doubted his word in anything. I doubt if any one ever heard him speak of the "Bell Witch" voluntarily; during his life the time did not seem proper to him.

He gave these recollections to me with the same admonition given to him by his father.

The Spirit talked to his father on the important topics of the day and told of happenings in the past of which no one had ever heard, and prophesied what was to be expected in the future, much of which has happened. My father knew many people, relatives, and friends who had talked to the Witch (?), but advised me that the confidential conferences between the Witch (?) and his father were the most amazing experiences to which any human being had ever been subjected; and not only the Bell family, but the whole world would finally be interested.

My father had no superstitious ideas. Of the many physicians who had him called in consultation and met him for years, not one ever had an idea of what he really thought of the Witch (?). He impressed them at once that he felt indignant any person of intelligence had ever called the visitor "Bell Witch", and that sometime it would be known what it was and he hoped it would be understood; that he was certain when it returned on its promised visit it would not be limited to the Bell family, but the whole country would share in the "honor" and he hoped they would profit by their experience.

My great Aunt Betsy Powell (daughter of John Bell) suffered great punishment from the Witch (?). I saw her when I was nineteen years old, while on a visit to Mississippi, where she lived with her daughter, Mrs. Zadok Bell. She was then about eighty-three years old. She gave me a most graphic account of the activities of the Witch (?). A chapter will be devoted to her experiences.

I have seen a number of reliable persons who came in contact with the Witch (?) and scores of others who had relatives and friends who heard its voice and witnessed its pranks. With the exception of Aunt Betsy, I did not ask for their experiences; they related it themselves. I shall write of what I have heard, leaving out the common "Witch" stories presented for the past hundred years.

More than forty years ago a book was published on the so-called "Bell Witch" which included a manuscript by Richard Williams Bell, a younger brother of John Bell Jr. My father and other members of the Bell family protested vigorously against this publication, not believing the time had come for any publication about the "Witch". My father declined emphatically to disclose anything he knew, telling me at that time his father's recollections when published were such as would give our most intelligent people an insight into the Spirit world.

He said that he thought Richard Williams' manuscript was true, but he was too young at the time to understand the Spirit, and certainly the Spirit could not disclose to him the wonderful things related to John Jr., who was, as the reader will learn, a man of intellect, courage, and indomitable will power. I will include such parts of Richard Williams' manuscript as I think of value, editing and leaving out things of least interest.

Neither John Bell nor John Jr., spoke of the Spirit as a Witch, but as a Spirit, which I shall designate it.

The Spirit made its final departure from the home of John Jr., assuring him it would return in one hundred and seven years.

I have read articles in newspapers and heard

from various sources that the Witch (?) would return in one hundred years, also that it was in the neighborhood for more than fifty years. The Bell family have regarded these statements as neighborhood "Witch tales". No member of the Bell family has seen or heard from the Spirit since it bade John Jr., farewell in 1828.

The Author will not write voluminously on Mentality, the Human Mind, the Soul, Spirit, and Philosophy, but will adhere to the facts as nearly as possible, giving some reasons why these statements can be true in the light of scientific investigations, and why the Bells called the mystery a Spirit; as to what kind of Spirit, John Jr.'s attack on the Spirit may give some insight.

The Author admits that he does not know the identity of this being, nor has he ever come in contact with any person who he believes knew anything more than it was a Spirit.

The fact that it came and remained four years, then went away returning, as promised, after seven years, left again and promised to return after one hundred and seven years, and no one could say from whence it came or where it went forces us to the conclusion that, whatever it was, we have never known of a greater mystery; and if its prophecies come true in the future as they have during the past one hundred years, then we have much yet of a spiritual nature to experience which we have thought human beings would never know in this world. That time is very much nearer at hand than it was fifty years ago. Things are happening now that were foretold to John Bell Jr., by the Spirit.

I believe, after reading a real account of the Spirit's visit to the Bell homes, one must know it was not just "superstition of the times." A person of reason likely would doubt that such performances could have been carried on by a human being. Could it be so performed at the present time, when we are so far advanced in sleight-of-hand, telepathy, and electricity?

Think of the excitement it would create! What is being done now of a seeming supernatural act is not comparable to some things the Spirit did more than one hundred years ago.

John Jr., instructed his son, J. T. Bell, that he was not to disclose what was said in his conferences with the Spirit, but to pass it on to his son and on to succeeding generations, until the time came when its publication would be of great value to the people of the country.

On account of the depression, from which so many thousands of our people are now suffering, and that so many church people are doubting the divinity of Jesus Christ, and that there is a heaven and hell, all of which the Spirit foretold, and the fact that the Spirit said it would be back in the year of 1935, I believe the reader will agree with me that my grandfather and father would both think now would be the proper time to publish these recollections. The Spirit prophesied that the only way for the world's recovery would be by spiritual improvement.

As to what citizens thought of the Spirit as an actual occurrence, I would only suggest that the reader may communicate with any descendant of the oldest Robertson County families—he will learn that for years the Spirit's visit was a most interesting subject of their thoughts and conversation; and to this day I would be surprised if there could be found a grown citizen of that county who could not tell tales of the "Bell Witch".

A Spirit is entirely separate from the material body, therefore some of the performances of the Spirit that visited the Bells have always been completely mystifying. That it brought fruits to members of the family and did many other things that were of a material nature has baffled everyone who has attempted a solution. Simply saying that these things were impossible and likely the products of superstition does not solve the mystery.

THE AUTHOR.

304 Chapel Ave., Nashville, Tenn.

CHAPTER I

A BIOGRAPHICAL SKETCH OF MEMBERS OF THE BELL FAMILY

This sketch of members of the Bell family is given that the reader may, in advance, become acquainted with certain members whose experiences while occurring, and for years after, created a nation-wide sensation; yet the most remarkable and most interesting conferences with the Spirit were kept from publication until now, for reasons deemed best for the family and the country.

Our real opinion of the reality of the Spirit's visit must be based upon the good sense, courage, integrity, and reputation for truth of these children of John Bell, whose recollections are written in this book.

John Bell was born in 1750, in Halifax County, North Carolina. He was a son of William Bell, who was of English descent, a man of high standing and a farmer of considerable wealth. For hundreds of years the Bells were a well known English family.

In 1782, John Bell married Lucy Williams, daughter of John Williams of Edgecomb County, North Carolina.

John Williams gave Lucy a young negro woman named Chloe and her son, Dean, as a bridal present. John Bell bought a farm in Edgecomb County which he managed in a thrifty way and accumulated wealth in land and slaves. Twenty-two years of happy married life found them with a family of six children; their first slave woman, Chloe, in the meantime had eight children.

John now decided to move to Robertson County, Tennessee, where he had a number of old friends who gave him a most happy reception. He bought one thousand acres of fine land on Red River near Adams, some four miles from the Kentucky line. The improvements at the time John Bell bought the land consisted of a large double log house, one and one-half stories high, with six large rooms and a large reception hall, and an ell consisting of several rooms and a large passage. The house was weather-boarded and had a wide porch across the front; it was among the best houses in the county at that time. There was a fine orchard in the rear of the house, and the front lawn was shaded by immense pear trees, which stood for more than a century. After Mrs. Lucy Bell's death the house for a time was unoccupied; finally, it was torn down and made into other buildings.

The land at this time is still very fine; at the present time the old homestead site belongs to

THE BELL WITCH

a great-grandson of John Bell, Judge John Bell Turner, former Chief Justice of Oklahoma, who returned to Tennessee a few years ago.

John Bell began at once to finish the improvements on the farm and clear more land; he built cabins for his negroes, barns for hay and tobacco, and stables for numerous horses and mules.

These were the days of the beginning of the Western emigration; some of the best families in Tennessee were among those in that community who had moved from the older States, east and north of Tennessee, and to this day their descendants rank among the best.

Neighbors at that time rendered each other every possible assistance, such as log rolling, barn raising, and hog killings. All these were the scenes of happy neighborhood meetings. The work was considered only as a joyous feature that brought them together. Tests of strength at lifting, shooting at turkey head targets, and riding unbroken horses were greatly enjoyed by the men; and for the youngsters, wrestling, running foot races, and shooting with bow and arrow featured these meetings.

The women vied with each other in the preparation of the dinners, which consisted of roast wild turkey, fish fresh from Red River, fine corn, salt-rising light bread, pies, cakes, and maple

THE BELL WITCH

syrup from nearby trees. The women usually had a quilting party on the same day.

After the day's work was over John Jr., always invited the negro slaves, as well as the friends, to partake of a generous drink of whisky which was made at the spring for family use only. No one was made drunk, but just "sharpened their ideas."

Churches were built; the first was the Red River Baptist Church, in 1791; this same organization, probably the oldest in this State, has a nice modern church at Adams. The next, a Baptist church at Drake's Pond, on the State line, about a mile of Guthrie, Ky. The Methodists also built several churches.

Without regard to which church they belonged, the people attended services at both churches, services alternating, Baptist one Sunday and Methodist the next Sunday. Prayer services were held on mid-week nights at John Bell's home and at James Johnston's.

At the time of the Spirit's arrival at John Bell's home the family consisted of John Bell; his wife, Lucy; and the following named children: Jesse, John Jr., Drewry, Benjamin, Esther, Zadok, Elizabeth, Richard Williams, and Joel Egbert.

Zadok became a lawyer of unusual ability, but

THE BELL WITCH

died at an early age in Alabama, where he had gone to practice his profession. Benjamin died when a child. The other seven lived to be citizens of high standing and successful in their vocations.

John Bell used his land in a very successful way, accumulating wealth in money and slaves. He was always generous in making loans to his neighbors, taking no mortgages and letting them have such amounts as they wished, which they invariably paid back.

John Bell's children chose neighborhood men and women when they married. Jesse, the oldest, married Martha Gunn, daughter of Rev. Thomas Gunn, a Methodist minister. Esther, the elder daughter, married Bennett Porter, July 24, 1817. A year or two after John Bell's death these two families moved to Panola County, Mississippi, and their descendants are numerous there today. The other sons became farmers, acquiring large tracts of land in the neighborhood.

A chapter will be devoted to the daughter, Elizabeth, whose tragic experience with the Spirit was of nation-wide interest. The recollections of John Jr. of the Spirit, which the author considers the most interesting ever heard or written, will be found in another chapter. The citizens who knew John Jr., regarded him first as a sol-

THE BELL WITCH

dier hero, then as a man who had the greatest regard for the best interest of his fellow men. Richard Williams' manuscript will also be given.

Drewry never married. He bought a large farm on the north side of Red River, opposite his father's farm, and led a lonely life, with only his slaves on the place. He lived a life of constant apprehension and was never left alone; he feared the return of the Spirit. He never recovered from the experience of seeing his father die, doomed to his death by the Spirit.

Joel Bell lived to an advanced age, first living on a part of the old home place, then bought a fine farm five miles north of Springfield. He was highly respected, a man of wealth and influence, and whose descendants are among the best people of Robertson County. Such recollections as Joel Bell had of the Spirit were that of a youngster, he being a child about four years of age when the Spirit arrived on its first visit and nearly nine when it left. He and Richard Williams were with their mother at the old home place when the Spirit returned in 1828; Joel was then about sixteen or seventeen years old and remembered the visit very well, and years afterward told of the return visit. Joel was, as stated, the youngest child.

He was at J. T. Bell's home very often, and

THE BELL WITCH

the author often visited at his home during his youthful days, but he heard him say very little of the Spirit. Knowing of the silent dispositions of the members of the Bell family, it was thought he preferred not to be questioned. The only recollection he gave was to corroborate a statement that the Spirit had advised his mother to give him a spanking, and when she failed to do so, the Spirit gave him a never to be forgotten spanking. He had just returned from a visit to his sister Betsy, who lived in Mississippi at that time, and he spoke of reminding her he still remembered the spanking and that Betsy remembered it quite well, too. He also remembered that Harry, the house-boy, was well whipped for being late getting in to kindle the morning fires, and many other things written in this book.

At the time of his death, John Bell owned many slaves, and these were divided among his heirs. The author saw some of these ex-slaves and heard them tell of the Spirit's activities and how the old negroes still remembered "Old Marster."

This is not a book on the "old Southern gentlefolks" or how they treated their slaves. A great many people in that county were of the gentlefolks of which so much has been written, but there were, as often happens, others who were

THE BELL WITCH

not quite so honorable; the Spirit's influence on the latter was quite marked for the better.

John Bell's tragic death, killed by the Spirit, as stated elsewhere, occurred December 20, 1820. It sent a shudder of horror through the people throughout the country. The funeral concourse was one of the largest ever known in the State at that time. The manner of his death will be described in a later chapter. He was buried by the side of his son, Benjamin, on a hill near the old home, where later his wife, Richard Williams, and Zadok were buried by his side.

Judge John Bell Turner, his great-grandson, who now owns this land, as already stated, one hundred and fourteen years after his death, reverences this spot and is proud of his lineage.

CHAPTER II

THE SPIRIT MAKES ITS APPEARANCE AT THE BELL HOME

The Bell family lived the usual happy life of a large country family, surrounded by everything the country afforded. Nothing of a disturbing nature occurred until they were firmly fixed in the attachment and confidence of their neighbors and friends.

Some twelve or fifteen years after their arrival in Tennessee, John Bell was going to the north end of the farm to look over the daily work and give such orders to the overseers as necessary. He carried his rifle, thinking possibly to get a shot at a rabbit, or a duck at the pond. As he passed the north end of the orchard, he saw a peculiar looking animal sitting between two corn rows. It looked like a dog, yet on closer inspection he could not determine to what species it belonged. He shot at the animal, which at once disappeared.

A short time later, Drewry and Betsy saw strange creatures for which they could not account; but as the country was new and many dif-

THE BELL WITCH

ferent animals and birds were seen, they did not attach much importance to what they saw.

About this time Betsy saw what she believed to be a woman strolling about the orchard; she spoke to her, but had no answer, the apparition at once disappearing. Sometime after Betsy, Drewry and their father saw these apparitions on the farm, the family began hearing queer noises at the house, as if someone was knocking at the doors and windows; also as if wings were flapping against the ceilings. On opening the doors, nothing could be seen to cause these outside noises. Soon the noises became greater on the inside. The sounds in the bedrooms appeared to be such as would be heard if the beds were suddenly and roughly pulled apart, to which was added fighting dogs chained together, making a noise most deafening and exciting. Betsy and the boys were very much frightened. Their sister, Esther, was married and not at the Bell home at this time. When lights were flashed upon the scene, the noises ceased, and not a thing out of the way could be seen, nor had any damage been done to the furniture.

These mild demonstrations continued for a year or more, increasing until the house fairly shook as if in a storm, and the noises could be heard at quite a distance. By command of John

THE BELL WITCH

Bell the family said nothing of these noises.

At first John Bell Jr., thought it might have been caused by the earth quaking, as there had been quakes several years earlier, but of course had ceased then. They knew, too, that they were the only people in the neighborhood whose home was so troubled; had it been general they would have heard of it without asking.

About this time John Bell developed a peculiar illness which affected his tongue and the muscles of his jaws; chewing and swallowing became difficult. This illness was attributed to the Spirit at this time. No doubt it was a disease of the nervous system which certainly may have been caused by the Spirit, but not in a direct manner, as supposed; simply, the continued annoyance had its effect on his nervous system. This disease in no way affected his thinking powers; he attended to his business and made financial deals as usual.

At this time he decided to seek counsel among his friends, hoping some suggestion from them might give him some relief. He asked one of his best friends, James Johnston, well known for his courage and Christianity, to come to his home and spend the night, telling him for the first time of the distressing condition.

Mr. Johnston readily agreed to do all he could

THE BELL WITCH

for him. He and his wife both came to pass the night in the Bell home. As usual, Mr. Johnston read a chapter in the Bible and prayed most earnestly for his friends in their time of trouble; after which he and his wife retired to their room adjoining Betsy's.

Soon unheard-of noises began, worse than ever, invading Mr. and Mrs. Johnston's room, stripping the covers from their bed, laughing loudly in a derisive tone, causing Mr. and Mrs. Johnston to become very much frightened. To all entreaties and demands for a reason for all this there was no answer, as to why it was there or from whence it came, there was no reply but loud laughter.

They all spent a sleepless night and if possible were further from a solution of the mystery than before.

Mr. Johnston advised John Bell to ask other friends' assistance in an attempt to fathom the source and cause of this uproar; to try to ascertain the motive for the demonstrations, which he agreed to do. There were selected a number of courageous and determined men, good friends of John Bell, who were almost constantly at his home from that time on until the Spirit left, striving in every way to induce this being to let it be known what it all meant. It continued much the

THE BELL WITCH

same actions as when Mr. and Mrs. Johnston spent the night at the Bell home.

After a few nights the Spirit voluntarily began to talk for the first time, beginning in almost a whisper. The first real talking was a repetition of Mr. Johnston's prayer and song given the first night he spent at the Bell home. So exact was this imitation, both in its repetition and sound of voice, it was said one could not tell it from Mr. Johnston's voice.

At this time the being, uninvited, played the part of host at the Bell home, entertaining the neighbors and people from the surrounding country; as could be imagined, its reputation became greater every day.

It assumed a pious character, apparently enjoying religious talks and quoting Scripture fluently with absolute accuracy. No preacher of that day could successfully argue Scripture with the Spirit; it often corrected them in their interpretations of Scriptural meanings, at times telling them of some differences in translations, pointing out what it insisted was the correct translations. No one could dispute very successfully these points.

It joined in the singing at the weekly prayer services with a voice, the sweetness of which was unsurpassed. People were attracted from great

THE BELL WITCH

distances to hear this singing; at times it sang songs never heard before in that country and never forgotten during the life of those who heard this wonderful singing.

It prayed with great fervor and eloquence, causing persons who heard it to believe that the world was about to become much better.

It must be understood that while the Spirit was displaying all these accomplishments, members of the Bell family and the best minds of the times were not idle, but were doing all in their power to solve the mystery. They were certain there was no accomplice, that no human being was either instrumental or aiding an outside force, that the being was there and actually engaged in exhibitions causing both doubts and astonishment in this country and in England; astonishment to those who witnessed the feats performed and doubts in the minds of those who only read or heard of it. No one who saw these actions and heard the Spirit talk was ever known to doubt the existence of a supernatural being of some kind.

As time passed, the Spirit was very ready to let itself be known to visitors at some time during their stay; and a visitor was rarely, if ever, disappointed in being able to see and hear all that he wished. The Spirit was active in its watch-

THE BELL WITCH

fulness of all events occurring in the neighborhood. Nothing was said or done of any moment that was not reported by the Spirit, and at once became well known far and wide. Under this espionage that community rapidly became a model in everything demanded of good citizens. The Spirit even knew the thoughts of those with whom it came in contact, and it did not hesitate to tell the evil thoughts of those so read at the Bell home.

People came from hundreds of miles on horseback and in covered wagons to witness these feats. These guests were never charged a cent for board or lodging, and were taken care of as long as the house would hold them. At length these visitors, on account of numbers, brought tents and occupied them.

Never at any time did the Bells and their friends, aided now by an occasional visitor from other states, cease their endeavors trying to discover what the Spirit meant and what it was after.

Finally it did answer, "I am a Spirit; I once was very happy, but have been disturbed." This was spoken in a voice quite distinct and understood by all present.

Immediately after the Spirit began talking, it asserted that it would remain and continue worrying John Bell, finally killing him; never explaining or giving any reason for this dislike.

It never at any time cast any reflections upon John Bell's character, or tried in any way to influence anyone to doubt his integrity, but continually reviled him and at times punished him severely with blows and other physical methods.

Joel, Betsy and Richard Williams were also punished by having their hair pulled, their jaws slapped, leaving red finger marks on their faces.

At none of these investigations were the "real scientific" persons who claimed they were going to expose the "Witch tricks" overlooked by the Spirit; they came in for a full punishment if they openly expressed doubts. Usually it followed these guests on their journey home for quite a distance, giving them final advice on the subject of "Witches" and inviting them back when they felt they could solve the mystery.

Betsy, the younger daughter of John Bell, who had attended the neighborhood school, had many friends among the students.

Her first sweetheart was one of her boy schoolmates, Joshua Gardner, a fine young fellow whose family was highly respected; but the Spirit opposed the union of these young people. No one has ever known for what reason, neither Betsy nor Joshua knew. The Spirit became so

THE BELL WITCH

abusive toward Betsy that she spent a great deal of time away from home with her girl friends.

Richard Powell, the young man who taught the school, was a teacher of fine reputation and a good friend of the Bell family. He was exceedingly worried that the Bell family was so persecuted by the Spirit.

A full account of these two friends of Betsy's, and her marriage to one will be given in the chapter devoted to Betsy and her trials. That the Spirit was the controlling factor, Betsy was forced to acknowledge. No matter if she were away from home with her girl friends, the Spirit followed her, nor did it forget those left at home, but continued the same actions which had now assumed a more abusive character than before, still religious, pious and prayerful, but at times displaying a frightful temper with all the family except Mrs. John Bell. Neither did it give John Jr., the same offensive treatment as it did the other sons.

The Spirit always declared Lucy Bell (John Bell's wife) the most perfect woman living, and never at any time displayed animosity toward her. It seemed to have a respectful regard for John Jr. While having sharp verbal encounters with him, it was never known to use physical force with him, and was always on the defensive when he bitterly assailed it; never for a single time restraining himself, but with the short, stern language for which he was noted he would quickly answer the Spirit. On account of this great respect for John Jr.'s mighty intellect, courage and sternness, the Spirit told him many things it never uttered to others. It said it was telling him of future events and many past events for that reason, knowing that he knew how to use such information in the best way. John Jr., was placed in a position in which all history has no record of a duplication; yet he must have acted for the best interest of his family, and the future generations of his countrymen.

He formed his opinion of and divined the nature of this being in a most philosophical way. It would seem that he really forced the Spirit to say the things told him in their conferences and verbal tilts. Never at any time did he show the least fear of the Spirit, but always denounced it in the most abusive terms, designating it as a "Spirit of the damned," not asking what it was, simply assuming that no other Spirit would perform such atrocious acts.

About this time a gentleman from England visited at the Bell home, remaining several months, with the expressed determination (made known only to John Jr.) of solving this mystery.

THE BELL WITCH

As stated in previous chapter, the Bells were of English descent; however, this may not have been the cause of the visit.

It was expressly understood that this visitor's name and residence were not to be made known by the family, which was readily agreed to. Strange to say, the Spirit made no announcement to outsiders giving the identity of this gentleman, but did some extra performances apparently for his enlightenment, telling him he would have some real tales to write up on his return to England, and "Be sure to get it all straight." The gentleman was highly entertained and experienced such performances as would satisfy the most skeptical of the absolute supernatural powers displayed.

During this time, at a Sunday night meeting at the Bell home, the Spirit repeated the sermon of Rev. James Gunn, preached at Bethel Methodist Church, for the benefit of those who had not attended the morning services. Rev. Gunn was present and his voice was imitated so that those present thought he must be talking; his text and prayers were given with exactness, he admitting it to be so.

Some one present said to the other preacher, Rev. Sugg Fort: "Brother Fort, you have the advantage; your sermon was not heard." The Spirit began at once repeating Rev. Fort's sermon and prayers in his voice and exact words, giving out hymns, etc. Rev. Fort said it was all correct. This performance was so astonishing that it left all present and all who have heard of it since in complete mystery.

The Englishman, about this time, was thinking in a most serious way of this, and many other things he had heard the Spirit say; the Spirit told him of his thoughts and that he was a sensible man to have remained, making no fuss and not saying the foolish things others had. It told him he was puzzled over the things he had seen and heard, and it would now give him another to think about. It told him within two or three hours he would hear from home, as usual (the Spirit had kept him informed as to what was going on at his home in England all this time, which the Englishman always learned was true when he received letters from his home) and asked him what he should tell the home folks; that it would convey any message to them he wished; this it had never done before.

The Englishman said, "Tell them that in my opinion, never since the world was created have men seen and heard the marvelous things I have witnessed during the past three months."

Within three hours a voice began repeating astonishment at what was being told them, and

THE BELL WITCH

another voice exclaimed incredulously, "Why, that is brother's voice; where are you, brother?"

The Englishman told John Bell and John, Jr., who were the only other persons present, that the voices were his mother's and brother's. (The Spirit had given a perfect imitation of their voices.)

The Spirit then gave their return message in the voice of the mother, "Tell him not to stay any longer; he has heard and seen enough, and we do not want any more visits like that here."

The Englishman knew his mother's voice, yet, to prove conclusively that it was she, he wrote John Jr., as soon as he arrived home that all that had been said was correct and that all who believed it were amazed, but few people believed it could actually have happened. John Jr.'s veracity was unquestionable, as will be seen in his recollections given to his son, J. T. Bell.

This incident actually occurred and was never told to any person other than to J. T. Bell, who was equally as silent on the subject of the "Bell Witch."

This Englishman saw and heard many things told of in the chapter devoted to the recollections of John Jr., and at no time after a thorough investigation did he doubt the supernatural origin of the manifestations exhibited. He went home

THE BELL WITCH

carrying with him an experience which has been handed down in that country for generations, and which will likely never be forgotten. It is not known with certainty at this time who the Englishman was; John Jr.'s assurance was that he was a high-class man and of great intelligence.

Other visitors from Europe were at the Bell home during the stay of the Spirit, but remained only a short time. None could offer further explanation than that it was a supernatural being, and no evidence other than to exclude a human being.

Frank Miles, one of John Jr.'s best friends, who was one of the most powerful men, physically, living at that time, was ever ready to aid the Bell family. He was present at the death of John Bell.

He was a man of some six feet two inches tall, weighed about two hundred and fifty pounds, with no surplus flesh, had a grip with his hands that would crush an ordinary man's hand, could perform wonderful feats of strength and was a man of undoubted courage.

Mr. Miles, like his friend, John Bell, did not hesitate to say if he could ever get the Witch (?) in his grip, he intended attempting to hold and crush it. Unlike John Jr., who knew it to be impossible to get a grip on the Spirit, he made such

THE BELL WITCH

attempts frequently while staying overnight at the Bell home.

Mr. Miles related that on extremely cold nights all the bed covers were quickly jerked off; the covers which he caught and held were torn wide apart and in pieces, leaving only small pieces in his hands. On two occasions the bedtick was snatched from under him and the bed rolled across the room by unseen force; he was unable to grasp the offender, but he said he felt the most forceful blows about his head and face he had ever had; while the Spirit kept up a most exasperating laugh, telling him "he was sure a strong man and could knock the wind out of the air, but not dangerous in a tussle with a Spirit."

Mr. Miles never faltered in attempting to be of assistance to the Bell family, and was present at many of the most interesting meetings when the Spirit was present. To his dying day, he was uncertain as to what region the Spirit came from, but he was certain that it *was* a Spirit that could display great strength and yet not be seen.

He was a good friend of Jushua Gardner and Richard Powell; he thought of Betsy as a sister. He sympathized heartily with them, and time and again repeated the heart-rending experiences of Betsy, which he personally saw, but could give her

THE BELL WITCH

only the comfort of his presence and heartfelt admiration for her great courage and endurance.

(The author, when a small boy, heard Frank Miles tell of many performances of the Witch which he had witnessed.)

CHAPTER III

RECOLLECTIONS GIVEN BY SOME OF THE SLAVES

John Bell's negro slaves had many "Witch" stories to tell, but on that subject it must be agreed that negroes' statements are as reliable as their scared state will allow.

Harry, the negro boy, some eighteen years old, came in the mornings to kindle the fires, which were all in open fireplaces. Wood was still being used when the present older members of the Bell family were growing up, and he often told them of some of the performances he saw and felt.

He was late getting in for a few mornings, his Master scolded him, and told him he must get in earlier; the very next morning Harry was late again, and while he was on his knees trying to blow the coals into a blaze, suddenly pieces of his kindling began beating him all over the body; finally he was jerked up across a chair and given such a beating that the blows were heard all over the house; while the beating was being administered Harry let out such yells and begged so for his life that John Bell was alarmed, fearing the

THE BELL WITCH

negro would be disabled. It then told Harry if he were ever late again he would be beaten to death and thrown into the fire. Harry was never late again.

He admonished his hearers not to tell Marster (J. T. Bell) what he had told, as he had been forbidden by "Old Marster" never to say anything of the Spirit.

The author heard the first of the Spirit from the lips of old Harry, who came to cut wood for the fires at J. T. Bell's home, many years afterward.

Old Uncle Harry (children called him Uncle "Hack") related, "When Missus Betsy wuz bout yo' gals' age, whut go wid de boys, dere wuz a boy tuk to cumin' to see huh; and Lawd a mercy, when I wuz makin' up dem fires, I heerd dat Witch talk de orfullest fore dem, just made Miss Betsy so shamed she haid to run outen de room, and dat boy wud go right on home; but he kep' cumin' back. Missus Betsy sho liked dat boy an' he jus' cudn't keep away from huh. Dat air Witch knowed dey wanted ter marry, hit kep' hollerin, 'Betsy, don't marry Joshua Gardner.' Now, I tells yo' hit scairt dem outen ever marryin'. I don't see how enybody cud er tried as long as dey did, mos' folks ud er quit dat very minit hit said, 'Don't you marry.' I cud see all dat

THE BELL WITCH

time dat Ole Marster wud be glad if dey jest naturly quit, but he never tol' dem to."

Uncle Hack said he saw his Old Marster's tracks in the snow a little while after he died, but no persuasion could induce him to expatiate on that occurrence. He would shake his head and say, "Dat wuz my young marse John's and de Witch's bizzness and not for me to tell. I jes' ain't gwine ter talk 'bout dat."

He told that one night after carrying in the kindling and wood for the next morning, he was on his way to his cabin when a voice commanded him, "Go right over to Mr. James Johnston's and cut wood and kindling for his morning's fires; he and his folks are sick and I told him I would send you. Step right on. James Johnston is the best man in this country. Your Master will be glad I sent you. Don't stop to ask him." Harry hurried to Mr. Johnston's home, some half a mile away; that gentleman told him the Spirit had promised to send him to get up the wood, just as it had said, and he felt very thankful that Harry came. The Spirit then asked Mr. Johnston if he wanted Harry to come next morning and kindle his fires, and said, "It will be no trouble, as Harry just likes to make fires on cold mornings. If you are going to be sick long, Harry will come every day and see to your fires; I'll tell his

THE BELL WITCH

Master to send him, and you know he will be glad to have it done." Others have told of this same occurrence.

At this time Uncle Hack told of the "Witch's" (the negroes always called it Witch) accuracy in "tellin' a pusson when de wether wud change, hit knowed dese suddin changes wuz cumin' an' if hit were gwine ter snow or rain. Lawd, chillun, young Marse John allus asked dat Witch if hit wuz gwine rain 'fore he cut down eny hay, an' ev'y day indurin' crop time he 'quired uf hit 'bout de wether, and hit kep, him tol' when to spect frost in terbacker cuttin' time; hit ud jest tell him how de col wether wuz goin' fur a long way fum heah, and when it ud hit us. Hit wuz mi'ty fine 'bout de wether, but nuthin' else." Harry always looked around to be certain of no danger of being heard before he made the last remark.

Many white persons and negroes have told of recollections of neighbors going to John Bell's during crop season to learn what the weather would be and in no instance were they misguided, for frost, rain, snow or continued fair and warm weather were accurately foretold.

Willis, a colored man who greatly assisted in the bringing up of J. T. Bell, was highly regarded by that gentleman, who was often heard to say, "If any man deserved a home in Heaven, it was

THE BELL WITCH

Willis." When Willis was about middle age, J. T. Bell, then a boy, taught him to read and write; then, later on, grammar and other school studies. Willis was an apt pupil; he soon began reading the Bible and became a preacher, a real one. Many years after the war he continued to come to the home of Dr. J. T. Bell to inquire after his and the family's health, and to express his continued appreciation and respect.

Willis was a neat, well-dressed man and spoke far more correctly than the average white man, and had the reputation of being an able preacher. He never spoke of the "Bell Witch." His training had been quite different.

Once, when visiting Dr. Bell, who at that time was looking over his father's (John Bell Jr.) recollections, Dr. Bell asked him some questions regarding his recollections of the Spirit. (The author's father then called him in as these things were to be passed on to him, and the two were having this most confidential conference.)

Willis told of the enmity toward negroes always, and of the experience of negroes who were afraid at the time to tell, but told him years after the Spirit had left. He said that Dean, John Bell's favorite slave, brought from North Carolina, was a favorite target for the Witch. Dean would come in at times during the coldest weather after a visit to his wife, who lived at Rev. Thos. Gunn's, with practically all of his clothes torn off, and with the appearance of having had a sound thrashing. The Spirit having had no mercy, but Dean said, "It jest wanted him to run."

Dean took his possum dog, Caesar, out for a night's sport. He soon treed a possum. Dean then cut down the small tree, in the top of which was the possum; he proceeded to cut off the top, splitting it and putting the possum's tail in the crack, expecting to leave him there until he caught another. Then came the Witch (?), drove the dog away with savage fury, and told Dean that was no way to treat even a possum. "Just like a nigger to do that," and began at once to administer a terrible beating, giving him a lick on the head with his own ax or stick and leaving him lying senseless for a time. Next morning his Master was uneasy when Dean did not make his appearance, and on going to his cabin found him in that condition. Dean carried that scar given by the Spirit the balance of his life; and after the Spirit was gone he had no fears of telling the facts, as told his Master the morning after the adventure. Dean had many adventures with the Spirit, but none so thrilling as this one. Many times did his son, Dean Jr., relate these contacts

THE BELL WITCH

with the Witch (?) to the youngsters of the succeeding generations.

The author heard Ibby tell this: Dean's wife's sister Ibby (Ibby and her sister lived at Rev. Thos. Gunn's), who lived to quite an advanced age, knew of Dean's troubles with the Spirit. She could scarcely be prevailed upon to tell of these escapades. Fifty years afterwards, she was still afraid of the Spirit and always said, "Better fur evabody to let the Sperrit go on and stay thar." She said that often Dean came in late at night almost breathless, with "nothin' but the whites of his eyes looking nateral like." The Spirit had talked terrible talk all the way, and she would often hear its parting advice, "Now, nigger, you'd better get your Master Jack Bell to buy your wife and quit running up here nights. You are just coming to see if any other niggers want her. Preacher Gunn don't want you 'round here every night." "Now, I tells yo' white folks no uther nigger cummed 'round, and I spicioned Dean cum and jes' tuck that chasin' to keep uther niggers 'way. It sho wuked. Mitey few niggers cum to our house, and sho nuff dere wuz mitey little running 'round at nite, fur nobody knowed whar dat Witch mout stop em on de road and ast questions, and give 'em a few licks."

Dean was with his Master for a short time ev-

THE BELL WITCH

ery night and saw much of his suffering. Ibby also was there at times, and they both thought John Bell's suffering was very great. They both knew the white folks of the neighborhood, and always in the evening saw some of them with the Bells.

Dean, on one occasion, as told by Ibby and Willis, was told by his Master to saddle and lead to the front a certain stranger's horse. He did so, and the stranger told Dean he had not seen a Witch and didn't believe the stories he had heard. As he mounted the horse the Spirit began telling him that it had been there all the time and had heard his talk. "Now, hold tight and see how far your horse throws you," it said. Then the horse gave a terrific snort, raised his back and began kicking and bucking. The man went into the air, landing on his all-fours, painfully hurt. The Spirit had all this time been calling to him to hold tight. Dean picked the man up and took him into the house, where he was laid out for the rest of the day, the Spirit taunting him for his disbelief. The horse was caught and the stranger left as soon as he was able to ride.

At the mouth of Sturgeon creek, where it empties into Red river, north of the Bell farm, was a celebrated baptizing place for the negroes; this was used for that purpose until comparatively

THE BELL WITCH

recent years, and white folks always attended. During the Spirit's reign it was always on hand.

At times the negroes were so scared that the ceremonies were all but broken up; then the Spirit would command them in a stern voice to stay right there and do their duty or it would follow them, throw them into the river and drown all those converted negroes, preacher and all. It joined in the singing; told them what songs to sing, and when a negro well known among his fellows as a real sinner was baptized, it would call out, "Parson, put him under again and keep him there a little longer." The parson always did it. Once in a while a negro would be a candidate for baptism who had been baptized two or three times. The Spirit would at once admonish such ones to make good this time, "the next time I catch you here I am going to have you drowned."

The Spirit quoted correct Scriptures to these negroes and assured them that their parson was a good man, and not to forget that they had been baptized; quit all their sins and be good to each other.

CHAPTER IV

THE SPIRIT'S KINDNESS AND HIGH REGARD FOR MRS. JOHN BELL

Mrs. John Bell was well known as a good woman, endowed with extraordinary intelligence. She brought her children up in a manner that impressed every one with their good behavior; and her children loved and respected her. Her neighbors and every one with whom she came in contact admired and had a high regard for her.

Much is said in Richard Williams Bell's manuscript of the treatment of his mother by the Spirit; this short chapter is to impress the reader that others had the same opinion of her and contributed their experiences, corroborating what was generally known; they having had the opportunity of knowing Mrs. Bell and seeing the Spirit's action toward her. Each one told of the Spirit's really affectionate actions toward her, always treating her with the greatest respect, no matter what humor it might display toward others.

Mrs. Bell did not antagonize the Spirit. She saw that would be futile, so she always spoke kindly of it and to it, thus hoping in some measure to influence a better treatment for her two loved ones, her husband and her daughter, Elizabeth, who were suffering greatly from its taunts and jeers, and other exceedingly painful actions. She could not influence the Spirit to better behavior toward her husband; at least, it seemed so extremely outrageous, that we could not think of it as possible to have been worse.

The Spirit always spoke to Mrs. Bell in a most respectful manner. It asked her many questions regarding her affairs, both household and financial, and offered advice it deemed best; to all of which Mrs. Bell listened and in most instances heeded.

The good and bad points of all of her neighbors were told to her, as well as those of her own children.

She had left many relatives in North Carolina whom she seldom saw and correspondence was slow, but the Spirit kept her informed of them as often as she liked. She was never afraid of the Spirit, so far as its treatment of her was concerned, but lived in constant fear of what further punishment it might inflict upon her husband and Betsy.

The Spirit often scolded Mrs. Bell's negroes and occasionally punished them for not doing

THE BELL WITCH

their work better, and told them that if it were not for fear of hurting their Mistress' feelings it would beat them almost to death. (This was told by the negroes themselves.)

Richard Williams Bell, in his account of the Spirit's treatment of his mother, was at a loss to understand why it treated her so differently from what it did his father and sister Betsy; the latter being a young girl against whom no one could conceive of a cause for prejudice. The neighbors and others who saw this could account for the lovely treatment accorded Mrs. Bell only that the Spirit was controlled by an unseen power directing it to in no way offer her personal mistreatment. These neighbors who knew the family so well, and believed Mrs. Bell to be such a good woman, also believed Betsy to be good, and esteemed John Bell just as highly.

These neighbors thought if it were a Spirit from Hell, as many really believed it was, such a Spirit could have been controlled by a greater Spirit. Mrs. Bell could have been endowed by her Creator with a Spirit and Soul that the cruel visitor had neither the power nor disposition to worry, she not realizing the source of her influence.

Mrs. Bell had her neighbors meet at her home for Bible study and for advancement of missions and those things accompanying church affairs.

THE BELL WITCH

The Spirit readily took part and when refreshments were served it always brought in nice fruits coming from they knew not where, but were simply dropped on the table or in their laps with the invitation to eat them. It joined in the singing with the voice that had become famous, volunteering a solo at times, singing songs none present had ever heard, but all agreed were sacred hymns of a most beautiful melody and words of wonderful composition.

At the old-time quilting parties, it was always on hand, giving these ladies directions how it should be done, but never discourteous on account of Mrs. Bell. Persons who were present at these meetings have said that the Spirit gave them information that was wonderful; at the church affairs it was ready to give them advice that no human being could have offered. Except at church meetings it always told them jokes on their husbands, leaving John Bell out of such, saying that "he was too dignified and precise in all things to do anything that might cause a laugh." It told these ladies that many men had been made to appear very foolish trying to find treasures, which it had pretended to exist; and again of how many silly things men had done attempting to find out who it was, and where it came from, always adding that whatever it was "Luce (it always called

THE BELL WITCH

Mrs. Bell Luce) would never have cause to personally fear it."

Mrs. Bell used every art she possessed to get the Spirit to tell her of itself. It told her that if it would tell any human being in this world she would be the one, but it would not tell her. It told her it would be here again after many years and that when it came, at that time people would imagine themselves so smart that they could easily comprehend what it was. It only laughed and said, "Luce, I wish you could be there and let yourself be known. Luce, you will see from where you are how this country develops and with your great goodness you will be sorely distressed at the way they have reached the position of envy to which they have climbed. Luce, I'll be there and you will be able to see what I do from where you are, and you will know exactly what I am, and why I am there."

In Richard Williams Bell's recollections an account is given of his mother's serious illness and of how attentive the Spirit was to her; of how it brought her fruits to eat and anxiously inquired how she was, and did wonderful things for her (other eye witnesses have told of this). One can not doubt that the Spirit was largely responsible for her recovery. It let her know of its anxiety

THE BELL WITCH

and wishes for her recovery, and she knew the Spirit expected her to get well.

When the Spirit returned to the old home place in 1828, after seven years absence, fulfilling a promised visit, Mrs. Bell absolutely expected it and did not feel that it would do any harm while there, which it did not. She said nothing of the Spirit's visit during the time it was at her home on this last visit, not wishing to alarm those of her children who were away from the old home. She did not know that the Spirit made a visit to her son John's home at this time, and of which no other of the older members of the family knew.

No matter what one's opinion would be of the reality of the Spirit visiting the Bells, there can be no doubt of the sublime character of Mrs. Lucy Bell. She underwent the loss of her husband, believing he had been killed by the Spirit, according to its own confession and evidence of all those present, after it had tormented him for more than four years.

She had seen her beloved daughter, Betsy, undergo frightful punishment, a fact to which some of the best people, preachers and laymen in Robertson County testified. Yet this noble woman emerged from it all still trusting and believing in Jesus Christ and that it all must some day prove to have been done for the best. She

THE BELL WITCH

never, at any time, doubted the goodness of her husband, and never thought it had been done for any sinful act.

She lived to see Betsy happily married; and a short time after the Spirit's return visit, she died and was buried by the side of her husband.

CHAPTER V

BETSY BELL'S TRYING EXPERIENCES WITH THE SPIRIT

Elizabeth was only twelve years of age when the Spirit made its appearance, and grew to young womanhood while it was a visitor at her home.

There have been persons who intimated that Betsy had something to do with the exhibitions of the Spirit, but nothing could have been further from the truth. She was too young, if so inclined, and too, when she was away from home the Spirit came there just the same. Sometimes it followed her to a neighbor's.

Such judgment has come into the minds of superstitious and naturally devilish people in all ages of the world, calumniating old women and young innocent girls.

Joan of Arc, according to history, was burned at the stake, after being tried by the English or their representatives, and found guilty of witchcraft and heresy, and she was only nineteen years old.

Some years later Joan was declared innocent by the Pope, and in May, 1920 (think of this, *only a few years ago*) she was enrolled as a saint by the Catholics. They were only too long doing this.

A bishop and other churchmen aided in the trials which finally ended in a verdict of burning at the stake.

Guizot's history of France relates of her, "That the same monk who was with her when she was burned at the stake, when questioned twenty-four years later at the rehabilitation trial, as to the last sentiments and the last words of Joan, said that to the very last moment she had affirmed that her voices were heavenly, and they had not deluded her; and that the revelations she had received came from God."

Certainly, one must lack reasoning power to believe that Joan of Arc, when under seventeen years of age, and with no military training, could have defeated the armies with which she contended, commanded by good generals, if she had not been given the power as she claimed.

When about thirteen years of age, she began hearing voices, telling her she could free her country and crown Charles king. These voices she described and told what was said; she told Charles that she knew a prayer which he had made, some years before, and repeated it to him. He knew no one had ever heard the prayer, so was convinced of Joan's mission and divine aid.

THE BELL WITCH

"What she said to him, there is none who knows," wrote Alan Chartier, a short time after (in July, 1429), but it is quite certain that he was all radiant with joy thereat as at a revelation from the Holy Spirit."

M. Wallon has given the following exposition of this mysterious interview. "Sire de Boisy," he says, "who was in his youth one of the gentlemen-of-the-bedchamber on the most familiar terms with Charles VII, told Peter Sala, giving the king himself as his authority for the story, that one day, at the period of his greatest adversity, the prince, vainly looking for a remedy against so many troubles, entered in the morning, alone, into his oratory and there without uttering a word aloud, made prayer to God from the depths of his heart, that if he were the true heir, issue of the House of France (and a doubt was possible with such a queen as Isabel of Bavaria), and the kingdom ought justly to be his, God would be pleased to keep and defend it for him; if not, to give him grace to escape without death or imprisonment, and find safety in Spain or in Scotland, where he intended in the last resort to seek a refuge. This prayer, known to God alone, the Maid recalled to the mind of Charles VII."

The never to be forgotten deeds and cruel death of Joan of Arc have been written of by emi-

THE BELL WITCH

nent writers; and great sculptors have given of their artistic talents to perpetuate her memory.

The French will for all time revere her sacred memory, not through the efforts of the artists, but the real facts recorded by great historians that—she claimed when a young girl to have heard voices of Angels directing her to deliver France from its enemies; that she so delivered France through divine directions, and only erred when, after repeated urging, she continued in the army after her work was completed. She herself had predicted that she would die. Her death was a blot upon those who caused it, from which they will never recover.

She, like Betsy Bell, was the daughter of a farmer, a girl of unusual good looks. She, like Betsy, was popular among her neighbors, a devout Christian and perfect character.

If Betsy had lived a comparatively short time earlier she might have been tried for witchcraft, and yet not the slightest reason for such action.

When a child, Betsy went to the forests, the fields, and the river with her brothers; she knew all the trees, poplars, oaks, gum, maples and all the others; she enjoyed the budding of the trees in the spring and loved their red and golden hues in the fall.

She gathered the wild flowers and knew all

THE BELL WITCH

the birds in the woodland. Her brothers taught her to shoot a rifle; she knew how to hitch the mules to a plow or wagon, and was a fine horseback rider. She really knew the joys of living in a new country.

Betsy continued at school until she acquired the usual education of that time. At school she had her girl and boy friends, among whom was Joshua Gardner, a young man of splendid appearance and of a fine family.

Joshua and Betsy grew up sweethearts, not outspoken, but with the shyness of childhood. A great love grew to a devotion rarely equaled.

The Spirit at all times opposed the attachment existing between Betsy and Joshua, and would beseech Betsy in the most weird voice, "Betsy, please don't marry Joshua Gardner."

It said so many things to Betsy and Joshua in the presence of their friends of a highly embarrassing nature that the girl in time became quite hysterical and worn out in despair.

Joshua did not falter; his great love was quite sufficient to keep his courage unabated, and he would insist that they should not allow the Spirit to govern their actions.

Betsy had serious forebodings, believing that the Spirit's unseen powers might mean great danger for them; what and how, she knew not. Her

THE BELL WITCH

love for Joshua was as great as his for her; she proved this by her determination to put off marriage until they knew better what the result might be. She did not wish to subject Joshua to some great ordeal, which might take place on account of their marriage; there could not have been exhibited a greater proof her love.

But one must not forget that she and Joshua were both young, and either or both had time to change. Human love, it must be remembered, may change, the cause may be the association with another.

Betsy never forgot young Gardner, but Richard Powell, who had been their teacher, was now a candidate for the legislature, and while canvassing the country for that office frequently visited the Bell family and their friends. He again saw Betsy and at once recognized that she had grown to be a young lady of wonderful beauty and rare personal charm; just as he had believed she would when a pupil of his in the neighborhood school.

Betsy was a blonde, with a beautiful figure, lithesome, perfect complexion, rosy lips, a cheery disposition, good sense, and a perfect character.

Richard had heard of Betsy's and Joshua's betrothal. He congratulated the young people and wished them the happiest life which he thought they would have. He did not conceal his love for

THE BELL WITCH

Betsy, yet at this time understanding the affairs of the young couple, it was far from his intentions to cause a breach in their feelings toward each other. He made no avowal of love to Betsy, but told each of these young people how fortunate they were, and left them to themselves.

Betsy had for several years undergone cruel treatment from the Spirit, yet at times had enjoyed her friends' company at her home with great appreciation.

She had parties, dancing the old-time dances and playing the usual games; the Spirit always being present and prompting. They had picnics in the woods and fishing during the summer, the Spirit advising them just what to do.

Of the happy times of the young people in the winter season, sleigh-riding was the most enjoyable affair. A snow fall was greeted by a full house of happy young people.

On most farms were what the men called slides made with runners selected in the forests from trees, some five to eight inches in diameter, with a natural quarter circle curve, some ten or twelve feet from the ground. The trees were nicely dressed and built over these runners some two and a half feet high was a floor. The farmers used these slides for hauling tobacco to the barns during the cutting season; hauling barrels of

THE BELL WITCH

water or hogs to the smokehouse, and hog feed to the hog pens. These slides were used as sleighs by the young people.

Betsy related that on one occasion the boys had left the sleigh at the front door while the horses were unhitched and taken to the stable to be fed, and the young people enjoyed their midday meal. She and the other girls, soon as the dinner was over, seated themselves on the sleigh for a ride just as the boys were leading the horses up to hitch to the sleigh.

The Spirit's voice cried out, "Hold tight when we get to the corner."

The sleigh started along at a good speed around the house, making the corners at such speed, and skidding so, they had difficulty in staying in. The girls were very much excited, but stayed with the sleigh; finally, it stopped after going around the house three times. The boys then hitched the horses to it and they had their ride around the neighborhood.

At times the Spirit became furious at Betsy; it would pull her hair, pinch and slap her cheeks, leaving the imprints of this punishment, then crying out, "I tell you, don't marry Jushua Gardner." Betsy corroborated these statements made by others, and could have filled a book with her own experiences.

THE BELL WITCH

An interesting happening Betsy told was the visit of General Jackson to the Bell home. This visit was generally known and there has been an account of it published, but it must be remembered that Betsy was there and her recollections of this distinguished visitor to her father's home are of extraordinary interest, told in her own language.

General Jackson and Betsy's brother were well acquainted, but John Jr. was not at home on the occasion of the General's visit.

Knowing of the many visitors to the Bell home, General Jackson thought it would be better to camp, so his party had a wagon loaded with a tent and camping outfit, and they follewed on horseback.

When the wagon was a short distance from the Bell home it suddenly stopped; the driver could not make his horses budge the wagon; all his yelling and whipping the horses were of no avail; the team was simply unable to start the wagon; not a wheel turned, although they were on level ground. The General examined the wagon and said there was no reason why the horses could not pull it; the driver again tried them without success. The General then shouted, "It is the Witch."

A voice called from the roadside, "They can go on now, General." Neither the General nor

THE BELL WITCH

the men with him could see any one, but distinctly heard the voice and its promise to see them that night.

Betsy said, as soon as her father saw General Jackson, he had him and the entire party come to the house and entertained them with a good dinner and stories of when the Indians were on the farm, and of the mounds and relics of the mound builders.

In the party was a man who claimed to be a real "Witch tamer," and he thought no witch would appear while he was present. The other members of the party had been bragging on him, and on his having the Witch (?) bluffed. He said his pistol was loaded with a silver bullet and he just wanted to try it out on this witch.

Finally, he dared the Witch out. The General was beginning to be impatient at the delay in the apppearance of the Witch, when suddenly the braggart jumped from his chair, grabbed at the seat of his trousers, and shouted, "Boys, I am being stuck by a thousand pins."

A voice spoke out, "I am in front of you; shoot." The man drew his pistol and tried to shoot, but it would not fire.

Then the voice cried, "It's my night for fun." Soon there was heard repeated slapping of the man's jaws, and he yelled, "It is pulling my nose

THE BELL WITCH

off." Making a break for the door, which flew open, he jumped out, running with all his speed toward the wagon, yelling every step, while the voice kept giving him all sorts of advice.

General Jackson fairly roared with laughter and told her father that he had never seen or heard of anything so funny and mysterious, and would like to stay a week, which he was invited to do.

Again the voice spoke, saying: "There is another fraud in your party, General; I'll get him tomorrow night. It is getting late. Go to bed."

The rest of General Jackson's party could not be prevailed upon to spend another night after that. They said no telling who would be the next victim.

General Jackson told them he knew this fellow was going to be shown up and he wanted to stay over, but by noon the party was at Springfield, twelve miles away. They never came back.

John Jr. saw General Jackson several times during the years following the visit, but as was his custom, he did not mention the visit to the General.

Betsy said: "When the Spirit became so tantalizing, filling my mind with horror and causing

THE BELL WITCH

me to become so nervous, my parents often sent me to a neighbor's to rest for a night.

My first night away from home was spent with Theny Thorn, one of my best girl friends. Nothing was heard until after we retired, which we did early. We locked the door to our room securely. Just as soon as we had retired there came a loud knocking on our outside door, which seemed to fly open, and a great gust of wind was felt. Then our bed quilts were snatched off. Theny sprang up at once and lit a candle; to our surprise the door was not open. We adjusted the bed clothes and lay down again.

Then a voice spoke very softly: "Betsy, you should not have come over here; you know I can follow you anywhere. Now get a good night's sleep." A soft hand patted my cheek, and the voice again assured us that we would not be disturbed any more that night.

We both were very much excited, but we lay quite still and after so long a time fell asleep. Next day Theny went home with me; my mother related that the Spirit had told her all about our experience and for her not to be alarmed, that we would rest well and be home next day."

On the river near the north boundary of the farm is a cave, in the bluff which is about three hundred feet high and almost perpendicular.

THE BELL WITCH

There is sufficient room at the front of the cave for parties to have lunches; below the cave the river makes a good fishing place, and we often fished there.

The cave became famous as the "Bell Witch Cave." None of us ever knew of the cave being occupied by the Spirit, but on our pleasure trips we always heard its voice on the river or in the cave.

There were beautiful stalactites in the cave. We often took candles and went back quite a ways to a big room some thirty feet high, with a kind of upstairs to it; after passing through this, the passage became small.

One time when we were "exploring the cave" one of the boys in the crowd came to a place where he had to get down on his knees and crawl; suddenly he went into a kind of quicksand deposit and soon became so jammed in he could not get out. His candle was out and no one could get to him; suddenly the big room and all parts of the cave were lit up as if from a big lamp.

A voice called out, "I'll get you out." The boy's legs were seized as if by strong hands and he was drawn out with a face full of mud and nearly suffocated.

We all agreed not to tell our parents of this

THE BELL WITCH

nearly fatal accident, but that night when the Spirit arrived at the usual neighborhood gathering at our home, it asked the parents of the boy if they had gotten the mud out of the boy's ears. Then it told them of his predicament in the cave and advised them to put a halter on him the next time so his companions could pull him out if he got stuck again.

When we fished in the river just below the cave, we often caught some very nice fish; other times the Spirit would not allow us any success at all, but kept the corks bobbing and had us constantly jerking the lines up when we did not have a bite, then laughing in great glee at the fun it was having.

On one of our fishing trips it told us that fishing was not a love-making affair, and not to get the notion that all you had to have was a hook and line to catch him. "Just the right bait is all that is needed."

"One Thanksgiving Day, Richard Williams, Joshua Gardner, Theny Thorn, Alex Gooch and I took the dogs out for a rabbit chase which we often enjoyed. Often at night we went fox hunting.

We were down in the flat bottom field east of the house when the dogs "jumped" a rabbit; the boys whooped at the dogs and the girls clapped

THE BELL WITCH

their hands; the rabbit took a circular route, going to the top of the nearby hill, then to the bottom. It had repeated this four or five times, all of us cutting across, attempting to head it off before we began to think it queer that the rabbit did not take to the bushes, or some hole. This continued until the dogs' tongues lolled out and we became very tired of the chase; then the rabbit scampered off out of sight, soon outdistancing the dogs, and was gone.

That night, the Spirit, as usual, joked with us, telling us among other things, "Josh sure can run like a dog. I almost had to dodge between his legs; that rabbit you were chasing was me. Ha, ha, ha."

Betsy told of a birthday party that she gave. She had invited a number of young people and all came. Of course the Spirit was there, and it took great interest in all their games and their refreshments.

"When the dinner was placed on the table, the Spirit called out, "I have a surprise for you; come and see it."

Suddenly there was placed on the table by unseen hands a large basket of fruits—oranges, bananas, grapes and nuts. The Spirit called out, "Those came from the West Indies. I brought them myself."

THE BELL WITCH

We were all breathless with astonishment. It bade us eat and be merry, and said that it would have brought a few bottles of rare wine, but it did not think the preachers would like for us to drink it. It said that it had acted as though it was drunk a few times and blown whisky about just to see what folks would say when they smelled it. It also said that those who had the most to say against whisky liked best to drink it.

We all ate the fruit and nuts, though at first some of the young people hesitated, thinking perhaps there was a trick of some kind to it."

"I shall never forget a horseback ride which Richard Williams, Rebecca Porter and I took one early summer day. We were all riding beautiful, spirited young horses; we rode to the bend of Red River, on the north side of the farm, where were magnificent poplar trees of great height, some six or eight feet in diameter.

In the river bend were the Indian mounds, where we often dug up relics, such as arrow heads, tomohawks, etc.

We were caught by a terrible storm after we arrived among these numerous trees; the wind bent the trees and carried away leaves; now and then limbs were blown off, some falling around us. Before we had left the house the Spirit told us not to go, that a storm was coming; however,

THE BELL WITCH

it had a way of saying that when we were going off (just as our father did when he wanted us to stay home) and told us many things to scare us that were not true.

Just as the storm came up it called to us to cross the river as quickly as possible, or some of us would be killed. We were quite ready to take this advice and quickly started for the river, as the limbs and leaves were beginning to fall.

The horses decided they would go home, and not cross the river. We could do nothing with them; they reared and snorted; they ran sideways, threw up their heads and plunged, and were entirely unmanageable. We were badly frightened.

A voice called out, "You little fools, hold tight now, and say nothing to the horses."

Suddenly the horses quit rearing and went straight to the river crossing, getting us completely away from the storm, no doubt saving our lives, as afterwards we saw numbers of these immense trees had been blown up and had fallen in every direction along the path we were trying to follow.

Betsy heard a conversation between the Spirit and John Johnston, in which Mr. Johnston tried in every way to get the Spirit to tell what it was and where it came from.,

THE BELL WITCH

It answered, "I am a Spirit from everywhere, Heaven, Hell, the earth; am in the air, in houses, any place at any time; have been created millions of years; that is all I will tell you, Mr. Johnston."

Mr. Johnston was at our home almost daily and tried in vain to get the Spirit to shake hands with him. It told him of many things of a neighborhood character; it also told him of his thoughts ,and what his neighbors were thinking.

It is well remembered how highly the Spirit regarded John's brother, Calvin; it went so far as to allow Calvin to hold its hand. Calvin said the hand felt soft and velvety, like a woman's hand." Betsy was present at this handshaking.

Betsy related the tragic scenes just preceding and at the time of her father's death. Her statements were practically the same as John Jr.'s and Richard Williams'.

She did not know anything about its return visit after an absence of seven years, as she was not told of it until several years later.

In answer to the question, if she were present when the Spirit repeated the sermons of the two preachers, which were delivered some twelve miles apart, she said she was there and would never forget the sensation created by this performance. There were, besides the two preachers, a number of as good men present as ever lived. She knew

THE BELL WITCH

the two preachers, Brothers Fort and Gunn, and had heard them preach often. She could not tell the difference between the Spirit's delivery and theirs; the same voices and same admonitions to their congregations. The preachers did not have to admit their services had been reproduced; all present knew it.

The Spirit complimented them on their fine sermons and gave them a few of its own views on their texts. It then told those who were present not to forget that it was worth a great deal to the community to have the services of these two preachers, and that they had gone to a great deal of trouble doing many good things for them.

Betsy said she did not know of any one in Robertson County who had not heard of this marvelous performance of the Spirit, and no one who had ever seen or talked to any of those present ever doubted it.

The Spirit attended church regularly and could always tell what the preacher said; not always agreeing with them, but at all times crediting them with the good they had done.

Several times it told of Brothers ——————— going to sleep during services; afterwards every one was careful not to go to sleep in church.

There were people in the neighborhood who had not attended church any too regularly; it an-

THE BELL WITCH

nounced at one of the Wednesday evening meetings at her home that if these people were not at church the following Sunday night it would lead in a missionary meeting the following Wednesday night at their home, and continue with each of these backsliders until they all started going to church. Useless to say, those named occupied conspicuous seats at the next Sunday services and were quite regular in attendance from then on.

It was quite true that it kept all actions of the neighborhood well known, whether good or bad; if a man came home drunk, all the neighbors knew it; if he scolded his wife, or whipped the children, it was told; soon such things became unknown in the neighborhood.

"Of all of our friends, none were thought of more highly than Frank Miles. Brother John and he would have died for each other without hesitation.

The treatment the Spirit gave me was resented as much by Frank as by my brother John.

As was well known, Frank was the most powerful man any of us ever saw, and just as fearless as any living man. He was very tender-hearted, and one time he said to me, "Come, sit by me, little sister; I have come to give you a good rest; nothing will bother you while I am here."

THE BELL WITCH

This seemed to exasperate the Spirit. It screamed: "You go home; you can do no good here." It then gave my hair such a jerk that my combs fell on the floor, and pinched my cheeks until they were red, and ached.

Frank fairly shook the house, stamping on the floor, and dared it to assume any shape so that he could get hold of it. He went into such a rage that (the first time I ever heard him curse) he swore terribly; the scene was terrifying in the extreme, as the Spirit kept screaming at him to mind his own affairs; that it had slapped him over before and to be careful or it would knock his block off.

Frank apologized to me, patted my cheek and talked baby talk to me, telling the Spirit that it was the biggest coward ever, to visit this earth to torture a child, little more than a baby, and said, "Why not work on me, you fiend of Hell?"

Frank soon learned it was of no avail to offer to champion me in a fight; it only made matters worse, so he no longer offered to fight, but would look at me with the most sympathetic glances and say the nicest things to me, always telling me how much he thought I was bearing with the greatest courage any child in the world could.

Frank was always tender and good to me and

THE BELL WITCH

to all the family. He was never forgotten by any of us, and as long as there are Bells in the world I hope they will never forget the man who I know meant what he said when he offered to fight a fiend of hell for the Bell family, even though he died on the spot."

Betsy said that she had always thought her mother was the best woman she ever knew, and always believed her father to be as good a man as ever lived. Never at any time had she seen any reason for the Spirit treating her father so cruelly. There was every reason for the good treatment of her mother, but why she herself had received the treatment given her, she was simply unable to understand.

Betsy said that from the time of the Spirit's arrival until its departure it did not act in an offensive way toward her mother. She saw all the nice foods it brought her, and heard the solicitous questions asked by the Spirit when her mother was ill.

The Spirit never failed a single day to tell her mother what her relatives in North Carolina were doing and how they all were.

It gave "Luce," as it called her mother, a complete recital of all events transpiring in the neighborhood. No secrets could be kept from it, and all were immediately told to "Luce."

THE BELL WITCH

A couple in the neighborhood, after they had retired behind closed doors with no one on the place but themselves, ventured to confide their opinions of the Witch (?) and the Bell family. The next night, at the usual gathering, the Spirit gave their full conversation and advised the company not to talk too much; it would always be told and if they had any thoughts of "Luce" other than good ones, to get them out of their minds, for that also would be known and told.

Often it would tell people who came to our home of their thoughts, giving them a full expression of things they had thought, but never intended telling.

Its greatest delight was to completely bewilder men who came to our home thinking the Witch (?) stories were all a joke. I have seen big, strong men jump from their chairs and yell with pain, becoming so frightened that they had to be helped out of the house. It was not imagination on their part, as the blows could be heard and spots seen on their faces where they had been struck. I certainly had every reason to know it was no fancy. I had slaps, pinches and all kinds of punishment given me. Every time one of our visitors asked me to tell of these "tales," implying that what he had heard was a Witch (?) tale, he would receive this terrible punishment and was told that was the best way to tell it, so he would remember and not continue to think it was "just a Witch tale."

Betsy said no one who ever visited at her home had any doubts that the Spirit's manifestations were beyond the power of any human to perform. She had seen many persons who came with an opinion already formed that it was all superstition and not much to it, but the more intelligent visitors quickly changed their opinions.

She said she remembered especially two gentlemen coming from Philadelphia who, upon their arrival, acted as though they expected to enter through a door as into a show and see the Witch (?). After spending a tiresome afternoon and evening, one of the men said to his companion, "We are a pair of fools to make a trip like this on what some other sucker has told us."

Without further introduction the Spirit appeared and in a very businesslike way began: "What do you gentlemen wish to see or hear? It would be of no value to you for me to tell you what is going on in your homes at this instant. You would not believe that. Suppose I tell you, as I have to some other 'suckers' about your past. Do not look so frightened; neither of you have been to jail. You two were at a big eastern school where your professor of philosophy was inclined

THE BELL WITCH

to believe in a Spirit and certain mental states of human beings, which put his classes to deep thinking. Now, that is why you are here. Professor ——— (naming the professor) was far ahead of the 'sucker' list."

The two gentlemen became excited at this and began asking such questions of a scientific nature as their excited condition would permit. They said the professor was just as the Spirit stated, and his name and the school were given correctly.

The Spirit said the professor had died about three years before, or most likely he would be here too. These gentlemen assented to all this. The Spirit gave them a very accurate history of their lives, told them exactly where they lived and, as it usually did with visitors from a long distance, told them how their home folks were and what they were doing. When these gentlemen left they were as firmly convinced as they could be of anything that a Spirit was at our home."

Betsy modestly confessed that she never had any idea what the being was; it completely overshot her. She could think of it only as a supernatural being which at times was almost unbearable in its treatment of her, but very good to her after her father's death. At that time she was treated with great tenderness which led her to believe she would no longer suffer from its terrible punishment. Every day during these few weeks of respite, it would advise her mother to watch after Betsy and try to make her happy, and would ask if it could not bring her some rare delicacy for her to eat, which it did many times.

It told Betsy about girls of other countries, of the kind of lives they lived; gave her descriptions of how people were living in the best social surroundings in America; and of some of the famous entertainments given both in Europe and America. It told of parades, of their bands, and described their caparisoned horses. Afterwards she saw the papers giving the descriptions and knew the Spirit was correct. The only difference was, it went further into such descriptions, giving a personal history of some of the participants, not given in newspapers. These personal descriptions were not always as complimentary as one would like.

Betsy had undergone such treatment that after her father's death she became more apprehensive than ever, fearing that the Spirit would make her destruction the object of its actions. The Spirit was very considerate for some time after her father's death, even seeming to sympathize with the family, especially with Betsy. This changed attitude was so encouraging that Betsy

THE BELL WITCH

again became her natural, cheerful, sweet self. All her friends and the family were thankful for her return to that joyous manner that gave every one a cheerful feeling with whom she came in contact.

She and Joshua Gardner had become more devoted than ever, and were almost at the point of supreme happiness; yet Betsy had remembrances which did not make her feel perfectly safe. Joshua was the same devoted lover, importuning Betsy to marry him now. One day while he and Betsy were discussing their marriage, the Spirit, in that same unearthly voice, pleaded, "Betsy, do not marry Joshua Gardner."

Thus began the same torment as before; the effect, after the respite and hope of never seeing or hearing the Spirit again, was most appalling and heart-rending.

One can think of the feelings of this young couple who deserved the best things of life, and whose romance was blighted by a fiend unknown, only as tormented by the visitations of some demon Spirit wandering on the earth to try and torment the souls of God's own people. The Almighty must have allowed its manifestations only as a proof of his own power, which power alone must have returned the Spirit to wherever it belonged; *where,* **we do not know.**

THE BELL WITCH

Betsy determined that she must not marry Joshua; that to do so would cause them both anguish, even the thoughts of which were unbearable. She felt the responsibility, therefore did what must have been the wise thing. She asked Joshua to release her from her promise to marry him, which he did with a feeling of the same great disappointment that she felt.

Betsy was the same loyal daughter, and continued to make the home life as cheerful as possible under the great trials to which she had been subjected.

The Spirit was very joyful over the determination of Betsy to give up Joshua; as to why it should have been so interested, no one has ever known.

Joshua and Betsy never saw each other again. He went to West Tennessee shortly afterwards and settled there for life, living to an honorable old age.

Betsy said many women had told her that had they been in her place, they would have married Joshua. They would not have allowed the Spirit to spoil their lives. Her opinion was, not having ever heard of any one in such a position, such opinions were not very positive. She felt that she would be doing Joshua an injustice; and, as time proved, she married a man of wonderful

THE BELL WITCH

character and had not at any time had cause to regret her decision. She knew had she married Joshua that they would have lived in dread, even if the Spirit had not actually punished them, which she and Joshua both believed it would have done.

Quite awhile after Joshua left, Richard Powell began a serious courtship with Betsy. Richard had been in the Legislature, and had acquired a popularity unexcelled in Robertson County. He was the same handsome and distinguished looking gentleman, but had now acquired a finish and polish rarely seen, and his reputation was perfect.

Betsy yielded to his love-making and they were married. He was many years Betsy's senior, but this fact proved to be a real guarantee of the wife's happiness; the husband taking all the ills of life to himself and not allowing her to assume responsibilities which might become burdensome.

Their married life was a happy one. In her old age she delighted telling the happy incidents of her comparatively short married life. Richard died about seventeen years after their marriage.

Sometime after his death she went to Panola County, Mississippi, to live with a daughter who

THE BELL WITCH

had married Zadok Bell, of that county. She lived to an old age, dying in 1890.

She was then a woman of good memory, and while entirely silent to strangers on the subject of the Spirit, she corroborated what is written in this book (except the recollections of John Jr. which had never been told her), answering such questions as were asked, with no tendency to exaggerate the Spirit's powers, nor attempt to say what it was.

She has highly respected descendants in Mississippi and Tennessee, who should feel a pride in their descent from Elizabeth and Richard Powell.

It would be difficult to find a history of any woman who had such thrilling and cruel experiences, yet was brave enough afterwards to live the happiest part of her life in the same county where it all occurred, never faltering, always disregarding the foolish gossip that at times attempted to connect her with the actions of the Spirit.

She was always ready to render any assistance to those attempting to solve the mystery. She at no time failed to show her great appreciation of her friends' sympathy, and these same friends recognized her worth and goodness, never **at any time failing her.**

CHAPTER VI.

RECOLLECTIONS OF RICHARD WILLIAMS BELL.

After settling on Red River in Robertson County, Tennessee, my father prospered beyond his expectations. He was a good manager and hard worker himself, making a regular hand on the farm. He indulged no idleness around him and brought up his children to work, endeavoring to make their employment pleasurable. Mother was equally frugal and careful in her domestic affairs, and was greatly devoted to the proper moral training of her children, keeping a restless watch over every one, making sacrifices for their pleasure and well being, and both were steadfast in their religious faith, being members of the Baptist Church, and set Christian examples before their children. Father was always forehanded, paid as he went, was never in his life served with a warrant or any legal process, and never had occasion to fear the sheriff or any officer of the law, and was equally faithful in bearing his share of whatever burden was necessary to advance morality and good society. In the meanwhile he gave all of his children the best educa-

THE BELL WITCH

tion the schools of the country could afford, Zadok being educated for a lawyer, while the other boys chose to follow agriculture. Jesse and Esther had both married, settled, and everything seemed to be going smoothly when our trouble commenced.

I was a boy when the incidents which I am about to record, known as the Bell Witch, took place. In fact, strange appearances and uncommon sounds had been seen and heard by different members of the family at times, some year or two before I knew anything about it, because they indicated nothing of a serious character, gave no one any concern, and would have passed unnoticed but for after developments. Even the knocking on the door, and the outer walls of the house, had been going on for some time before I knew of it, generally being asleep, and father believing that it was some mischievous person trying to frighten the family, never discussed the matter in the presence of the younger children, hoping to catch the prankster.

Then, after the demonstrations became known to all of us, father enjoined secrecy upon every member of the family, and it was kept a profound secret until it became intolerable.

Therefore, no notes were made of these demonstrations, or the exact dates. The importance

THE BELL WITCH

of a diary at that time did not occur to any one, for we were all subjected to the most intense and painful excitement from day to day, and week to week, to the end, not knowing from whence came the disturber, the object of the visitation, what would follow next, how long it would continue, nor the probable result. Therefore, I write from memory such things as came under my observation, impressing my mind, and incidents known by other members of the family and near neighbors, to have taken place, and are absolutely true. However, I do not pretend to record the half that did take place, for that would be impossible without daily notes, but will note a sufficient number of incidents to give the reader a general idea of the phenomena and the afflictions endured by our family.

As before stated, the knocking at the door and scratching noise on the outer wall, which continued so long never disturbed me, nor was I frightened until the demonstrations within became unendurable. This, I think, was in May, 1818. Father and mother occupied a room on the first floor; Elizabeth had the room above, and the boys occupied another room on the second floor; John and Drewry had a bed together, and Joel and myself slept in another bed. As I remember, it was on a Sunday night, just after the family had retired, a noise commenced in our room like a rat gnawing vigorously on the bedpost. John and Drewry got up to kill the rat, but the moment they were out of bed the noise ceased. They examined the bedstead, but discovered no marks made by a rat. So soon as they returned to bed, the noise commenced again, and thus it continued until a late hour, or some time after midnight, and we were all up a half dozen times or more searching the room all over, every nook and corner, for the rat, turning over everything, and could find nothing, not even a crevice by which a rat could enter.

This kind of noise continued from night to night, and week after week, and all of our investigations were in vain; the room was overhauled several times, everything moved and carefully examined, with the same result. Finally, when we would search for the rat in our room, the same noise would appear in sister Elizabeth's chamber, disturbing her, and arousing all the family.

And so it continued, going from room to room, stopping when we were all up, and commencing again so soon as we returned to bed, and was so exceedingly annoying that no one could sleep. The noise was, after a while, accompanied by a scratching sound, like a dog clawing on the floor, and increased in force until it became evidently too

THE BELL WITCH

strong for a rat. Then every room in the house was torn up, the furniture, beds and clothing carefully examined, and still nothing irregular could be found, nor was there a hole or crevice by which a rat could enter, and nothing was accomplished beyond the increase of our confusion and evil forebodings. The demonstrations continued to increase, and finally the bed coverings commenced slipping off at the foot of the beds, as if gradually drawn by some one, and occasionally a noise like the smacking of lips, then a gulping sound, like some one choking or strangling, while the vicious gnawing at the bedpost continued, and there was no such thing as sleep to be thought of until the noise ceased, which was generally between one and three o'clock in the morning. Some new performance was added nearly every night, and it troubled Elizabeth more than any one else. Occasionally, the sound was like heavy stones falling on the floor, then like trace chains dragging, and chairs falling over.

I call to mind my first lively experience, something a boy is not likely ever to forget. We had become somwhat used to the mysterious noise, and tried to dismiss it from mind, taking every opportunity for a nap. The family had all retired early, and I had just fallen into a sweet doze when I felt my hair beginning to twist, and then a sudden jerk, which raised me. It felt like the top of my head had been taken off. Immediately Joel yelled out in great fright, and next Elizabeth was screaming in her room, and ever after that something was continually pulling at her hair after she had retired to bed. This transaction frightened us so badly that father and mother remained up nearly all night. After this, the main feature in the phenomena was that of pulling the cover off the beds as fast as we could replace it; also continuing other demonstrations.

Failing in all efforts to discover the source of the annoyance, and becoming convinced that it was something out of the natural course of events, continually on the increase in force, father finally determined to solicit the cooperation of Mr. James Johnston, who was his nearest neighbor and most intimate friend, in trying to detect the mystery, which had been kept a secret within the family up to this time. So Mr. Johnston and wife, at father's request, came over to spend a night in the investigation. At the usual hour for retiring, Mr. Johnston, who was a very devout Christian, led in family worship, as was his custom, reading a chapter in the Bible, singing and praying. He prayed fervently, and very earnestly, for our deliverance from the frightful disturbance, and that its origin, cause and purpose might be revealed. Soon after

THE BELL WITCH

we had all retired, the disturbance commenced as usual; gnawing, scratching, knocking on the wall, overturning chairs, pulling the cover off of beds, etc., every act being exhibited as if on purpose to show Mr. Johnston what could be done, appearing in his room, as in other rooms, and so soon as a light would appear, the noise would cease and the trouble begin in another room. Mr. Johnston listened attentively to all the sounds and capers, and that which appeared like some one sucking air through the teeth, and smacking of lips, indicated to him that some intelligent agency gave force to the movements, and he determined to try speaking to it, which he did, inquiring: "In the name of the Lord, what or who are you? What do you want, and why are you here?" This appeared to silence the noise for considerable time, but it finally commenced again with increased vigor, pulling the covers from the beds in spite of all resistance, repeating other demonstrations, going from one room to another, becoming fearful. The persecutions of Elizabeth were increased to the extent that excited serious apprehensions. Her cheeks were frequently crimsoned as by a hard blow from an open hand, and her hair pulled until she would scream with pain. Mr. Johnston said the phenomena was beyond his comprehension; it was evidently preternatural or supernatural, of

THE BELL WITCH

an intelligent character. He arrived at this conclusion from the fact that it ceased action when spoken to, and certainly understood language. He advised father to invite other friends into the investigation, and try all means for detecting the mystery, to which he consented, and from this time it became public.

All of our neighbors were invited and committees formed, experiments tried, and a close watch kept, in and out, every night, but all of their wits were stifled, the demonstrations all the while increasing in force, and sister was so severely punished that father and mother became alarmed for her safety when alone, and the neighboring girls came almost every night to keep her company. Especially were Thenny Thorn and Rebecca Porter very courageous and kind to her in this trying ordeal. It was suggested that sister should spend the nights with some one of the neighbors to get rid of the trouble, and all were very kind to invite her. In fact, our neighbors were all touched with generous sympathy, and were unremitting in their efforts to alleviate our distress, for it had become a calamity, and they came every night to sit and watch with us. The suggestion of sending Elizabeth from home was acted upon. She went to different places, James Johnston's, John Johnston's, Jesse Bell's and Ben-

THE BELL WITCH

nett Porter's, but it made no difference, the trouble following her wherever she went with the same severity, disturbing the family where she went as it did at home, nor were we in any way relieved. This gave rise to a suspicion in the minds of some persons that the mystery was some device or stratagem originated by sister, from the fact that it appeared wherever she went, and this clue was followed to a logical demonstration of the mistake, satisfying all who entered into the investigation.

After Mr. James Johnston expressed his opinion that there was an intelligent cause behind the manifestations, other persons commenced speaking to the Witch, as it was then called, importuning it to talk and tell what it wanted. When spoken to, it was observed that the noise would cease for a time, and then appear still more demonstrative. This conduct went to confirm Mr. Johnson's opinion, and investigators persisted with interrogations. By this time the mystery had gained wide notoriety, and people came from every direction, the house being crowded every night with visitors, who came to witness the demonstrations, and neighbors persevered in their efforts to induce the Witch to talk, calling on it to rap on the wall, smack its mouth, etc., and in this way the phenomenon was gradually devel-

THE BELL WITCH

oped, proving to be an intelligent character. When asked a question in a way that it could be answered by numbers, for instance, "how many persons present, how many horses in the barn, or how many miles to a certain place?" the answers would come in raps, like a man knocking on the wall, the bureau, or the bed post with his fist, or by so many scratches on the wall, like the noise of a nail or claws, and the answers were invariably correct. During the time it was not uncommon to see lights like a candle or lamp flitting across the yard and through the field, and frequently when father, the boys and hands were coming in late from work, chunks of wood and stones would fall along the way as if tossed by some one, but we could never discover from whence, or what direction they came.

In addition to the demonstrations already described, it took to slapping people on the face, especially those who resisted the action of pulling the cover from the bed, and those who came as detectives to expose the trick. The blows were heard distinctly, like the open palm of a heavy hand, while the sting was keenly felt, and it did not neglect to pull my hair and make Joel squall as often.

The phenomena continued to develop force, and visitors persisted in urging the Witch to talk, and

THE BELL WITCH

tell what was wanted, and finally it commenced whistling when spoken to, in a low broken sound, as if trying to speak in a whistling voice, and in this way it progressed, developing until the whistling sound was changed to a weak, faltering whisper, uttering indistinct words. The voice, however, gradually gained strength in articulating, and soon the utterances became distinct in a low whisper, so as to be understood in the absence of any other noises. I do not remember the first intelligent utterance, which, however, was of no significance, but the voice soon developed sufficient strength to be distinctly heard by every one in the room. This new development added to the sensation already created. The news spread, and people came in larger numbers, and the great anxiety concerning the mystery prompted many questions in the effort to induce the Witch to disclose its own identity and purpose. Finally, in answer to the question, "Who are you and what do you want?" the reply came, "I am a Spirit; I was once very happy, but have been disturbed." This was uttered in a very feeble voice, but sufficiently distinct to be understood by all present, and this was all the information that could be elicited for the time.

The next utterance of any note that I remember occurred on a Sunday night, when the voice

THE BELL WITCH

appeared stronger, and the Witch talking more freely, in fact, speaking voluntarily, and appeared to be exercised over a matter that was being discussed by the family. Brother John Bell had for some time contemplated a trip to North Carolina to look after father's share of an estate that was being wound up, and was to start next morning (Monday) on horseback, and this was the matter that interested the family and was being discussed, the long, tiresome journey, his probable long absence, the situation of affairs, concerning which father was giving him instructions. Several neighbors were present, taking an interest, volunteering some good-natured advice to John, when the Witch put in, remonstrating against the trip, dissuading John from going, predicting bad luck, telling him that he would have a hard trip for nothing, that the estate had not been wound up, and could not be for some time, and he would get no money, but return emptyhanded. As a further argument to dissuade John the Witch told him that an elegant young lady from Virginia was then on her way to visit friends in Robertson county, who would please him, and he could win her if he would stay; that she was wealthy, possessing forty negroes and considerable money. John laughed at the revelation as supremely ridiculous, and left on the following

THE BELL WITCH

morning, as contemplated, and was absent six months or more, returning empty-handed, as predicted. Very soon after his departure the young lady in question arrived, and left before his return, and John never met her.

The Witch continued to develop the power of articulation, talking freely, and those who engaged in conversation with the invisible persevered in plying questions to draw out an explanation of the mystery, and again the question was pressed, inquiring, "Who are you and what do you want?" and the Witch replied, stating the second time, "I am a Spirit who was once very happy, but have been disturbed and made unhappy." Then followed the question, "How were you disturbed, and what makes you unhappy?" The reply to this question was, "I am the Spirit of a person who was buried in the woods near by, and the grave has been disturbed, my bones disinterred and scattered, and one of my teeth was lost under this house, and I am here looking for that tooth."

This statement revived the memory of a circumstance which occurred some three or four years previously, and had been entirely forgotten. The farm hands, when engaged in clearing a plot of land, discovered a small mound of graves, which father supposed to be an Indian burying ground, and worked around it without obliterating the marks. Several days later Corban Hall, a young man of the neighborhood, came to our place and was told by Drew the circumstance of finding the Indian graves. Hall thought probably the graves contained some relics which Indians commonly buried with their dead, and proposed to open one and see, to which Drew agreed, and they proceeded to disinter the bones. Finding nothing else, Hall brought the jawbone to the house, and while sitting in the passage he threw it against the opposite wall, and the jarring knocked out a loose tooth, which dropped through a crack in the floor. Father passed through the hall in the meantime and reprimanded the boys severely for their action, and made one of the negro men take the jawbone back, replacing all the disinterred bones and filling the grave. This was evidently the circumstance referred to by the "Spirit," so long forgotten, and to be reminded of the fact so mysteriously was very perplexing, and troubled father no little. He examined the floor just where the bone dropped when it struck the wall, as the boys had left it, and there was the crack referred to, and he was pestered, and decided to take up a portion of the floor and see if the tooth could be found. The dirt underneath was raked up, sifted and thoroughly examined, but the tooth

THE BELL WITCH

was not found. The Witch then laughed at father, declaring that it was all a joke to fool "Old Jack."

The excitement in the country increased as the phenomena developed, the fame of the Witch had become widely spread, and people came from all quarters to hear the strange and unaccountable voice. Some were detectives, confident of exposing the mystery. Various opinions were formed and expressed; some credited its own story, and believed it an Indian spirit; some thought it was an evil spirit, others declared it was witchcraft, and a few unkindly charged that it was magic art and trickery gotten up by the Bell family to draw crowds and make money. These same people had stayed as long as they wished, enjoyed father's hospitality, and paid not one cent for it, nor did it ever cost any one a half shilling. The house was open to every one that came; father and mother gave them the best they had, their horses were fed, and no one allowed to go away hungry; many offered pay and urged father to receive it, insisting that he could not keep up entertaining so many without pay, but he persistently declined remuneration, and not one of the family ever received a cent for entertaining.

Father regarded the phenomena as an affliction, a calamity, and such accusations were very

THE BELL WITCH

galling, but were endured. Inquisitive people continued to exercise all of their wits plying the Witch with questions concerning its personality or character, but elicited no further information until the question was put by James Gunn, then came the reply, "I am the spirit of an early immigrant, who brought a large sum of money and buried my treasure for safe keeping until needed. In the meantime I died without divulging the secret, and I have returned in the spirit for the purpose of making known the hiding place, and I want Betsy Bell to have the money." The Spirit was then urged to tell where the money was concealed. This was refused and the secret withheld until certain pledges were made that the conditions would be complied with. The conditions were that Drew Bell and Bennett Porter would agree to exhume the money and give every dollar to Betsy, and that "Old Sugar Mouth" (Mr. James Johnston) would go with them and see that the injunction was fairly discharged, and that he should count the money and take charge of it for Betsy. The story was questioned and laughed at, and then discussed. The Witch had made some remarkable revelations, and it was thought there might be something to it, and the proposition was acceded to. Drew and Bennett agreed to do the work, and Mr. Johnston consented to become the

THE BELL WITCH

guardian and see that the right thing was done. The Spirit then went on to state that the money was under a large flat rock at the mouth of the spring on the southwest corner of the farm, on Red River, describing the surroundings so minutely that there could be no mistake.

Every one was acquainted with the spring, having frequented the place, but no one could have described it so minutely, and this all tended to strength faith in the revelation. The Spirit insisted that the committee selected should start very early the next morning at the dawn of day, lest the secret should get out and some fiend should beat them to the place and get the money. This was also agreed to, and by the break of day next morning all hands met and proceeded to the spring. They found everything as described, the huge stone intact, and were sure they were on time. They observed that it was an excellent place for hiding money, where no human being would ever dream of looking for a treasure, or care to move the great stone for any purpose, and yet susceptible of such a minute description that no one could be mistaken in the revelation. They carried along an axe and mattock, and were pretty soon at work, devising ways and means for moving the big rock, which was so firmly imbedded in the ground. It was no light job, but they cut

THE BELL WITCH

poles, made levers and fixed prizes, after first removing much dirt from around the stone, so as to get under it. Then Drew and Porter prized and tugged, Mr. Johnston occasionally lending a helping hand, and after half a day's very hard work the stone was raised and moved from its bedding, but no money appeared. Then followed a consultation and discussion of the situation. They reasoned that the glittering treasure was possibly sunk in the earth, and the stone imbedded over it to elude suspicion, and they decided to dig for it, and went to work in earnest, Porter digging and Drew scratching the loosened dirt out with his hands, and so on they progressed until they had opened a hole about six feet square and nearly as many feet deep, and still no money was found. Exhausted and very hungry, they gave up the job, returning to the house late in the afternoon much disgusted and chagrined. That night the "Spirit" appeared in great glee, laughing and tantalizing the men for being so easily duped, and describing everything that occurred at the spring in a most ludicrous way, telling how they tugged at the big stone, and repeating what was said by every one. Bennett Porter staved the mattock in up to the eye, every pop, and oh, how it made him sweat! It told how "Old Sugar Mouth" looked on prayerfully, encouraging the boys. The dirt

THE BELL WITCH

taken out was mixed with small stones, gravel, sand, etc., leaves and sticks, all of which indicated that the earth had been removed and put back. Drew, the Witch said, could handle a sight of dirt, his hands were made for that purpose, and were better than a shovel; no gold could slip through his fingers.

The Witch's description of the affair kept the house in an uproar of laughter, and it was repeated with equal zest to all newcomers for a month.

There were but very few churches in the country at this period of the century, nevertheless ours was a very religious community. Most of those coming from the older States brought their religion with them, and inculcated the principle in their families. The influence of Rev. James and Thomas Gunn, Rev. Sugg Fort, Mr. James Johnston, and other good men, swayed mightily. Every man erected an altar in his own home, and it was common for neighbors to meet during the week at one or another's house for prayer and exhortation and Bible study. In the absence of the preachers, Mr. James Johnston was the principal leader in these exercises, and the meetings were held alternately at his house and father's, and occasionally at one or the other of the Gunns. There was no spirit of denominational jealousy existing, and all Christians mingled in these meetings like

THE BELL WITCH

brethren of the same faith. The Witch, as it accumulated force, dissembled this spirit, giving wonderful exhibitions of a thorough knowledge of the Bible and Christian faith. The voice was not confined to darkness, as were the physical demonstrations. The talking was heard in lighted rooms, as in the dark, and finally in the day at any hour. The first exhibition of a religious nature was the assimilation of Mr. James Johnston's character and worship, repeating the song and prayer, uttering precisely the same petition made by the old gentleman the night he and his wife came for the purpose of investigation, and the impersonation of Mr. Johnston was so perfect that it appeared like himself present. It was not uncommon after this for the Witch to introduce worship by lining a hymn, as was the custom, singing it through and then repeat Mr. Johnston's prayer, or the petitions of some one of the ministers. It could sing any song in the hymn books of that time, and quote any passage of Scripture in the Bible from Genesis to Revelation. The propensity for religious discussions was strongly manifested, and in quoting Scripture the text was invariably correctly cited, and if any one misquoted a verse they would be promptly corrected. It could quote Scripture as fast as it could talk, one text after another, citing the book, chapter and number of the verse. It was common test to open the Bible at any chapter, and call on the Spirit to repeat a certain verse, and this was done accurately, as fast as the leaves were turned from one chapter of the book to another. It delighted in taking issue on religious subjects, with those well versed in Scripture, and was sure to get the best of the argument, being always quick with a passage to sustain its point. This manifest knowledge of Scripture on the part of the Witch was unmistakable, and was the most mystifying of all the developments, and strangers who came from a long distance were eager to engage the seer in religious discussions, and were no less astounded when the Witch would remind them of events and circumstances in their history in a way that was marvelous. Just here one circumstance I shall call to mind. The discussion had turned on the command against covetousness and theft. A man, whose name I will call John, put in, remarking that he did not believe there was any sin in stealing something to eat when one was reduced to hunger, and could not obtain food for his labor. Instantly the Witch perniciously inquired of John "if he ate that sheepskin." This settled John. He was dumb as an oyster, and as soon as the subject was changed he left the company, and was conspicuously absent after that. The result was the

THE BELL WITCH

revival of an old scandal, so long past that it had been forgotten, in which John was accused of stealing a sheep-skin. This warlock was indeed a great tattler and made mischief in the community. Some people very much feared the garrulity of its loquacious meddling and were extremely cautious, and it was this class whom the invisible delighted in torturing most. Nothing of moment occurred in the country, or in any family, that was not reported by the Witch at night. The development of this characteristic led the people to inquire after the news and converse with the Witch as they would with a person, very often inquiring what was transpiring then at a certain place or house in the neighborhood. Sometimes the answer would be, "I don't know; wait a minute and I will go and see," and in less than five minutes it would report and the report was generally verified. This feature of the phenomena was discovered in this way: Brother Jesse Bell lived within one mile of the homestead. He had been absent several days on a trip and was expected home on a certain evening. After supper mother entered the room, inquiring if any of us knew whether Jesse had returned or not. No one had heard, or could inform her. The Witch manifested much regard for mother on all occasions, and never afflicted her in any way. On this occasion it spoke promptly, saying, "Wait a minute, Luce; I will go and see for you." Scarcely a minute had elapsed when the voice reported that Jesse was at home, describing his position, sitting at a table reading by the light of a candle. The next morning Jesse came to see us, and when told the circumstance, he said it was true, and just at that time there was a distinct rap on his door, and before he could move, the door opened and closed immediately. His wife, he said, noticed it also, and asked him what had caused it, and he replied that he reckoned it was the Witch.

Every Sabbath service that occurred within the bounds was reported at night, the text, hymn, etc., and the preacher also criticised, and everything of peculiar note was described. The company was treated one night to a repetition of one of Rev. James Gunn's best sermons, preached in the vicinity, the Witch personating Mr. Gunn, lining the hymn, quoting his text and prayer, and preaching so much like Mr. Gunn that it appeared the minister himself was present. A number of persons were present who attended the meeting that day, and recognized the declamation as the same sermon. Shortly after this Rev. James Gunn preached on Sunday at Bethel Methodist Church, six miles southeast, and Rev. Sugg Fort filled his appointment at Drake's Pond Baptist

THE BELL WITCH

Church, seven miles northwest, thirteen miles apart, both preaching at the same hour, eleven o'clock. It so happened that both ministers came to visit our family that evening, finding quite a crowd of people gathered in, as was the case every day during the excitement. Directly after supper the Witch commenced talking as usual, directing the conversation to Brother Gunn, discussing some points in his sermon that day. Mr. Gunn asked the Witch how it knew what he had preached about. The answer was, "I was present and heard you." This statement being questioned, the vociferator began, quoted the text and repeated the sermon verbatim, and the closing prayer, all of which the preacher said was correct. Some one suggested that Brother Fort had the advantage of the Witch this time, that having attended Brother Gunn's service, it could tell nothing about Brother Fort's discourse at Drake's Pond. "Yes, I can," was the prompt reply. "How do you know?" was the inquiry. "I was there and heard him." Then, assuming Rev. Fort's style, it proceeded to quote his text, and repeated his sermon, greatly delighting the company. There was no one present who had heard either sermon, but both ministers admitted that their sermons had been accurately reproduced, and no one could

THE BELL WITCH

doubt the fact, or were more greatly surprised than themselves.

The reader will understand that no feature of the exhibitions already introduced was ever abandoned, but continued developing virulence, or beneficence and felicity. The practice of pulling the cover off the beds was a favorite pastime, and frequently the sheets would be pulled from under the sleepers, or the pillows jerked from under their heads, and other performances added to the exhibitions. The most mysterious consequence, however, was the afflictions of Elizabeth and father. Notwithstanding the invisible agency feigned a tender regard at times for Betsy, as it affectionately called her, it did not cease tormenting her in many ways, increasing her punishment. The feint pretext for this was a manifest opposition to the attention paid her by a certain young gentleman, who was much esteemed by the family, often interposing impertinent objections, urging that these mutual relations be severed. At least there was no other cause manifested, or this would not be mentioned. Sister was now subjected to fainting spells followed by prostration, characterized by shortness of breath and smothering sensations, panting as it were for life, and becoming entirely exhausted and lifeless, losing her breath for nearly a minute between gasps, and

THE BELL WITCH

was rendered unconscious. These spells lasted from thirty to forty minutes, and passed off suddenly, leaving her perfectly restored after a few minutes, in which she recovered from the exhaustion. There is no positive evidence that these spells were produced by the Witch. However, that was the conclusion, from the fact that there was no other apparent cause. She was a very stout girl, and with this exception, the personification of robust health, and was never subject to hysteria or anything of the kind. Moreover, the spells came on at regular hours in the evening, just at the time the Witch usually appeared, and immediately after the spells passed off the mysterious voice commenced talking, but never uttered a word during the time of her prostration. In the meantime, father was strangely afflicted, which should have been mentioned in the outset, but he had never regarded his trouble as of any consequence until after sister recovered from the attacks just described. In fact, his ailment commenced with the incipiency of the Witch demonstration, or before he recognized the phenomenal disturbance. He complained of a curious sensational feeling in his mouth, a stiffness of the tongue, and something like a stick crosswise, punching each side of his jaws. This sensation did not last long, did not recur very often, or

THE BELL WITSH

cause pain, and therefore gave him but little concern. But as the phenomenon developed, this affliction increased, his tongue swelling against his jaws, so that he could neither talk nor eat for ten or fifteen hours.

In the meanwhile, the Witch manifested a pernicious dislike for father, using the most vile and malignant epithets toward him, declaring that it would torment "Old Jack Bell" to the end of his life. As father's trouble increased, Elizabeth was gradually relieved from her severe spells, and soon recovered entirely from the affliction, and never had another symptom of the kind. But father was seized with another malady that caused him much trouble and suffering. This was contortions of the face, a twitching and dancing of his flesh, which laid him up for the time. These spells gradually increased, and undoubtedly carried him to his grave, of which I will have more to say further on.

People continued to ply our loquacious visitor with shrewd eager questions, trying to elicit some information concerning the mystery, which were with equal dexterity evaded, or a misleading answer given. First, it was a disturbd spirit hunting a lost tooth. Next, a spirit that had returned to reveal the hiding place of a buried treasure. Then it told Calvin Johnston that it was the spirit

THE BELL WITCH

of a child buried in North Carolina, and told John Johnston that it was his stepmother's Witch. At last Rev. James Gunn manifested a very inquisitive desire to penetrate the greatest of all secrets, and put the question very earnestly.

The Witch replied, saying that Brother Gunn had put the question in a way that it could no longer be evaded, and it would not do to tell the preacher a flat lie, and if the plain truth must be known, it was nobody else and nothing but "Old Kate Batts' witch," determined to torment "Old Jack Bell" out of his life. This was a startling announcement, and most unfortunate under the circumstances, because too many were willing to believe it, and it created a profound sensation. Mrs. Kate Batts was the wife of Frederick Batts, who was terribly afflicted, and she had become the head of the family, taking charge of her husband's affairs. She was very eccentric and sensitive. Some people were disposed to shun her, which was still more irritating to her sensitive nature. No harm could be said of Mrs. Batts. She was kind-hearted, and a good neighbor toward those she liked. Mr. Gunn, of course, did not believe the Witch's statement, nor did any of the Bells.

The Witch manifested a strong aversion for the negro, often remarking, "I despise to smell a

THE BELL WITCH

nigger; the scent makes me sick," and this no doubt accounts for the fact that the negroes were never molested in their cabins after night, but away from their quarters they encountered a sight of trouble. The Witch's repugnance was mutual; all the negroes disliked the Witch, and were careful to evade all contacts possible by staying in after night, augmenting that natural odor peculiar to the race, which was now worth something. They were afraid of the Witch, and it was difficult to get one out for an emergency. This fear was increased by the miraculous stories told by Dean, who was a kind of autocrat among the darkies, and, by the way, was a good negro, father's main reliance for heavy work, and noted for his skill with the axe, maul and wedge. He was worth two ordinary men in a forest clearing. Dean could see the Witch any time when alone, or on his way to visit his wife, who belonged to one of the Gunns. It appeared to him, he said, in the form of a black dog, and sometimes had two heads, and at other times no head. The negroes would stand around him with eyes and mouth wide open to hear his description of the Witch, his encounters and hair breadth escapes.

He always carried his axe and a "Witch-ball" made by his wife, according to Uncle Zeke's direction, to keep the Witch from harming him. He

THE BELL WITCH

came up one morning, however, rather worsted, with his head badly bruised and bloody, and always declared that the Witch inflicted the wound with a stick. Dean's stories are not to be quoted as altogether reliable; he was allowed a wide range for his vivid imagination. Harry, the house boy, however, had cause for believing every word Dean told. It was Harry's business to make the morning fires before daylight. He became negligent in this duty and father scolded and threatened him several times. Finally, the Witch took the matter in hand, speaking to father, "Never mind, Old Jack, don't fret. I will attend to the rascal the next time he is belated." This passed off like much of the gab, but a few mornings after, Harry was later than ever and father commenced scolding harshly, when the Witch spoke again: "Hold on, Old Jack; didn't I tell you not to pester? I will attend to this nigger." Harry had just laid the kindling wood down and was on his knees blowing the coals to a blaze when some unseen force apparently seized him by the neck and frailed him unmercifully. Harry yelled and begged piteously, and when let up the Witch spoke, promising to repeat the operation if he was ever derelict again. Father said he heard the blows as they fell with force, sounding like a paddle or strip of wood, but could see nothing but the boy

THE BELL WITCH

on his knees yelling for life. Harry was never late after that.

A rather funny trick was played on Phyllis, a twelve-year-old girl who waited in the house and assisted her mother in the kitchen. We had a log-rolling on our place, as was the custom in the country. After the work was over, the youngsters, while waiting for supper, engaged in some gymnastics, trying the difficult feat of locking their heels over the back of their neck. Phyllis observed these exercises and the next day stole up stairs to test her athletic capacity. After several unsuccessful attempts, she suddenly realized that her feet had forcibly gone over her head and were securely locked. Time and again, Aunt Lucy, her mother, called and Phyllis as often answered up stairs, but never came. Finally, Aunt Lucy got her "dander" up, and picking up a switch started, saying, "Bound I fetch that gal down sta'rs." Pretty soon there was a racket up stairs and Aunt Lucy had worn out the switch before Phyllis could explain that the Witch had her.

The case of Anky, however, lends more zest to the Witch's characteristic antipathy for the negro. Mother had taken notice of the fact that the Witch never made any demonstrations in the cabins and conceived the reason why, accepting the Witch's own statement. She exercised her

THE BELL WITCH

genius and hit upon a scheme to outwit the Witch, which was rather novel in its purpose. However, she turned the matter over in her own mind carefully, and spoke not a word about it, not even to father, for the reason perhaps that she was afraid of the thing, and believed she fared best by cultivating the regard it manifested for her, consequently no one knew a breath of her plans until the outcome of the scheme was developed.

Anky was a well-developed, buxom African girl, some eighteen years of age—a real negro, so to speak, exuberant with that pungent aromatic which was so obnoxious to the Witch's olfactory.

Mother had determined to cautiously test her plan for getting rid of the Witch, telling Anky in her gentle, patronizing way, that she wanted her for a house girl, and desired that she should sleep in her room. The girl manifested some misgivings, but felt complimented by the distinction implied, and inquired of mother if she reckoned the old Witch would not pester her? Being assured that there was not much danger, that the Witch would be too busy entertaining the company to take any notice of her, her fears gave way to her plucked-up courage, and she followed mother's directions to the letter, keeping the whole matter a secret from the other negroes and all the family until the test was made as to whether the Witch would trouble her or not. So one evening after supper, Anky quietly slipped into the room with her pallet and spread it under mother's bed, fixing herself comfortably on it, to await the coming of visitors and the Witch and hear the talking. It was a high bedstead, with a fringed counterpane hanging to the floor, hiding Anky completely. She was delighted and not a soul except mother knew she was there. Very soon the room was filled with visitors, keeping up a lively chit-chat while waiting the coming of the Witch, and mother had taken a seat with the company, anxiously waiting to see the outcome of her scheme.

Presently, the voice of the Witch angrily rang out above the din of conversation, with the exclamation, "There is a damn nigger in the house; it's Ank; I smell her under the bed, and she's got to get out."

In an instant a noise was heard under the bed like that of a man clearing his throat, hawking and spitting vehemently, and Anky came rolling out like a log starting down hill, her face and head literally covered with foam like white spittle. She sprang to her feet with wonderful agility, frantically exclaiming, "Oh, missus, missus; it's going to spit me to death. Let me out; let me out," and

THE BELL WITCH

she went yelling all the way to the cabin: "Let me in; let me in."

The Witch then addressed mother, "Say, Luce, did you bring that nigger in here?"

"Yes," mother replied, "I told Anky that she might go under my bed, where she would be out of the way, to hear you talk and sing."

"I thought so," replied the Witch. "I guess she heard me. Nobody but you, Luce, would have thought of such a smart trick as that, and if anybody else had done it, I would have killed the damn nigger. Lord, Jesus, I won't get over that smell in a month."

The Johnston brothers, John and Calvin, perhaps had more intercourse with the Witch than any other two men who visited our place during the excitement. That is, they talked more with the invisible, entered more earnestly into the investigation by cultivating friendly and intimate relations. They were both very honorable men, of high standing in the community, but were very dissimilar in character. Calvin was a plain, unassuming man of strict integrity, free from deception, faithful in everything he pretended, and would not swerve from the truth or break a promise knowingly and willfully under any circumstance. John was more dexterous, of a shrewd, investigating turn of mind, guided by policy, and would make use of all legitimate means at hand to gain a point or accomplish a purpose, and he cultivated the Witch more than any one else for the purpose of facilitating his investigations. The Witch was very fond of gab, and John Johnston made use of every opportunity to engage the Witch in conversation, hoping to draw out something that would give a clue to the mystery, but it appears that all his wits were baffled, and that the seer was all the while aware of his purpose.

The question arose as to the character of the blows received by so many persons on the cheek after retiring. The sound was like a slap of the open hand, and every one testified that it left a sting like that of a hand, even to the prints of the fingers being felt.

Calvin Johnston conceived the idea of asking the Witch to shake hands with him. After much persuasion, the Witch agreed to comply with the request, on the condition that Calvin would first promise not to try to grasp or hold the hand that would be laid in his. This he agreed to, and then holding out his hand, in an instant he felt the pressure of the invisible. Mr. Johnston testified that he felt it very sensibly, and that the touch was soft and delicate like the hand of a lady, and no one doubted his statement.

John Johnston begged the Witch to shake

THE BELL WITCH

hands with him, persisting that he was as good a friend as his brother, but the Witch refused, telling John, "No; you only want a chance to catch me." John vowed that he would not attempt anything of the kind. The Witch still refused, replying, "I know you, John Johnston; you are a grand rascal, trying to find me out, and I won't trust you."

Two or three other persons claimed to have shaken hands with the Witch, which I don't know about, though many testified to the force of the hand as felt on the cheek.

It was not uncommon for the Witch to recognize strangers the moment they entered the house, speaking to them on familiar terms. Here is one instance I will note:

Four strangers who had traveled a long distance (whose names I cannot now remember, there were so many unknown callers), arrived late on a dark night, and knocking at the door, they were admitted. They were unknown to any one in the house or on the place, but the moment they entered the door, and before they could speak to introduce themselves, the Witch announced one by name, exclaiming, "He is the grand rascal who stole his wife. He pulled her out of her father's house, through a window, and hurt her arm, making her cry; then he whispered

THE BELL WITCH

to her, "Hush, honey, don't cry; it will soon get well." The strangers were greatly confused. They stood dumbfounded, pausing some time before they could speak. The gentleman was asked before leaving if the Witch had stated the facts in regard to his matrimonial escapade. He said, yes, the circumstance occurred, just as stated.

A good-looking stranger arrived who introduced himself as Mr. Williams, a professional detective, stating that he had heard much of the Witch mystery, which no one could explain, and having considerable experience in unraveling tangled affairs and mysteries, he had traveled a long distance for the purpose of investigating this matter, if he should be permitted to do so; further stating that he did not believe in either preternatural or supernatural things, and professed to be an expert in detecting jugglery, sleight-of-hand performances, illusions, etc., and would certainly expose these manifestations so much talked of if given a fair chance. Father bid the gentleman a hearty welcome, telling him that he was just the man he wanted.

"Make my house your home, and make free with everything here as if your own, as long as you think proper to stay," said father. Mr. Williams politely accepted the invitation and hung up his hat. Mr. Williams was rather a portly, strong-

THE BELL WITCH

muscled, well-dressed, handsome gentleman. He was no less self-possessed, and wise in his own conceit, full of gab, letting his tongue run continually, detailing to the company his wonderful exploits in the detective business, and was very sure he would bring the Witch to grief before leaving. A day and night passed and the Witch, for some cause best known to the Witch, kept silent, making no show except a little scratching on the walls and thumping about the room, just enough to let the company know that the spirit was present. Mr. Williams became very impatient, appearing disgruntled, and spoke his mind more freely.

He said to a coterie of gentlemen who were discussing the Witch that he was convinced that the whole thing was a family affair, an invention gotten up for a sensation to draw people and make money, and the actors were afraid to make any demonstrations while he was present, knowing his profession and business, and that he would most assuredly expose the trick. One of the gentlemen told father what Williams had said, and it made him very indignant. He felt outraged that such a charge should be made without the evidence, by a man professing to be a gentleman, to whom he had extended every courtesy and hospitality, and had proffered any assistance he might call for, and in a rage he threatened to order Wil-

THE BELL WITCH

liams from the place immediately. Just at this juncture, the Witch spoke: "No you don't, Old Jack; let him stay; I will attend to the gentleman and satisfy him that he is not so smart as he thinks."

Father said no more, nor did he take any action in the matter, but treated Mr. Williams as gentlemanly as he did others, nor was anything more heard from the Witch. The house was crowded with visitors that night, all expectant and anxious to hear the Witch talk, and sat till late bedtime awaiting the sound of the mystifying voice, but not a word or single demonstration of any kind was heard from the Witch. This confirmed the detective in his conjectures, and he repeated to several visitors his conclusions, declaring that the Witch would not appear again as long as he remained.

After they were all tired out, mother had straw mattresses spread over the floor to accommodate the company. Mr. Williams, being the largest gentleman present, selected one of these pallets to himself. All retired and the light was extinguished, and a night of quiet rest was promising. As soon as perfect quiet prevailed, and every one appeared to be in a doze of sleep, Mr. Williams found himself pinioned, as it were, to the floor by some irresistible force from which he was utterly

THE BELL WITCH

powerless to extricate himself, stout as he was, and the Witch scratching and pounding him with vengeance; he yelled out to the top of his voice, calling for help and mercy. The Witch held up long enough to inquire of the detective which one of the family he thought had him, and then let in again, giving him an unmerciful beating, while the man pleaded for life. All of this occurred in less than two minutes, and before a candle could be lighted, and as soon as the light appeared the pounding ceased. The Witch did a good deal of talking, more than Mr. Williams cared to hear. The detective was badly used up and the worst scared man that ever came to our house. He sat up on a chair the balance of the night, with a burning candle by his side, subjected to the Witch's tantalizing sarcasm, ridicule and derision, questioning him as to which of the family was carrying on the devilment, how he liked the result of his investgations, how long he intended to stay, etc. As soon as day dawned, Mr. Williams ordered his horse, and could not be prevailed upon to remain until after breakfast.

William Porter was a very prominent citizen of the community, a gentleman of high integrity, regarded for his strict veracity. He was also a good friend to our family, and spent many nights with us during the trouble, taking his turn with

THE BELL WITCH

others in entertaining the Witch, which was necessary to have any peace at all, and also agreeable to those of an investigating turn of mind who were not afraid, and this was Mr. Porter's character; like John Johnston, he rather cultivated the Spirit, and said he was fond of gabbing with the Witch. This seemed to please the Witch, and they got along on good terms. William Porter was at this time a bachelor, occupying his house alone. The building was a large hewn log house, with a partition dividing it into two rooms. There was one chimney having a very large fireplace, and the other end was used for a bedroom—entered by a door in the partition.

I give this as related by Mr. Porter himself, to a large company at father's, and as he has often repeated the same to many persons, and no one doubted his truthfulness.

He said, "It was a cold night and I made a big log fire before retiring, to keep the house warm. As soon as I got in bed I heard scratching and thumping about the bed, just like the Witch's tricks, as I thought, but was not long in doubt as to the fact. Presently I felt the cover drawing to the back side, and immediately the Witch spoke, when I recognized the unmistakable voice of the Witch.

THE BELL WITCH

"Billy, I have come to sleep with you and keep you warm."

I replied, "Well, if you are going to sleep with me, you must behave yourself."

I clung to the cover, feeling that it was drawing from me, as it appeared to be raised from the bed on the other side, and something snakelike crawling under. I was never afraid of the Witch or apprehended that it would do me any harm, but somehow this produced a kind of chilly sensation, a freak of all-overishness that was simply awful. The cover continued to slip in spite of my tenacious grasp, and was twisted into a roll on the back side of the bed, just like a boy would roll himself in a quilt, and not a strip was left on me.

I jumped out of bed in a second, and observing that the Witch had rolled up in the cover, the thought struck me, "I have got you now, you rascal, and will burn you up." In an instant I grabbed the roll of cover in my arms and started to the fire, intending to throw the cover, Witch and all in the blaze. I discovered that it was very weighty and smelled awful. I had not gone halfway across the room before the luggage got so heavy and became so offensive that I was compelled to drop it on the floor and rush out of doors for a breath of fresh air. The odor emitted from the roll was

THE BELL WITCH

the most offensive stench I ever smelled. It was absolutely stifling, and I could not have endured it another second. After being refreshed, I returned to the room and gathered up the roll of bed clothing, shook them out, but the Witch had departed and there was no unusual weight or offensive odor remaining, and this is just how near I came to catching the Witch."

Major Garaldus Pickering, who was a distinguished man of that day, kept a large school near by which Joel and I attended, and we had many little experiences with the Witch along the way.

The custom was to take in school as soon as the teacher could get there, a little after sunrise, and dismiss about thirty minutes before sunset.

Our route was through the woods, and some briar patches and hazel thickets by the wayside. Passing these thickets, returning home, sticks of wood and rocks were often tossed at us, but never with much force, and we soon learned not to fear any harm from this pastime, and frequently cut notches on the sticks, casting them back into the thicket from whence they came, and invariably the same sticks would be hurled back at us.

After night the Witch would recount everything that had occurred along the way. Even if one of us stumped a toe, falling over, the Witch claimed to have caused it, and would describe how

THE BELL WITCH

it appeared in the form of a rabbit or something else at certain places. Our most serious trouble, however, was experienced at home, the Witch continually pulling the cover off and twisting our hair, and it was hard for a tired boy to get any sleep.

It happened that Joel and I were left to occupy a room alone one night, and were troubled less than usual in the early part of the night, but the Witch put in good time just before day. It was quite a cold morning, and rather too early to get up, but the Witch continued pulling the cover off and jerking my hair, and I got out of bed and dressed myself. Joel, however, was much vexed and said some ugly things about the Witch, and gathering up the cover from the floor, he rolled himself up in it for another nap. Directly the Witch snatched it from him again. Joel became enraged, pulling at the cover while the Witch seemed to be hawking and spitting in his face, and he had to turn the cover loose. This made Joel raving mad, and he laid flat on his back kicking with all his might, calling the Witch the meanest kind of names.

"Go away from here, you nasty old thing," he exclaimed. The Witch became furious also, exclaiming, "You little rascal, I'll let you know who you are talking to."

THE BELL WITCH

That moment Joel felt the blows falling fast and heavy, and no boy ever received such a spanking as he got that morning, and he never forgot it. It was absolutely frightful. I could do nothing for his relief. He yelled frantically with all of his might, arousing the whole house, nor did his punisher cease spanking until father entered the door with a light, finding him almost lifeless.

The blows sounded like the spanking of an open heavy hand, and certainly there was no one in the room but Joel and myself, and if there had been, there was no way of escaping except by the door which father entered, and that would have been impossible unobserved.

The Shakertown people at that time kept their trading men on the road continually traveling through the country, dealing with the people. They went in twos, generally on horseback, and could be distinguished from other people any distance by their broad brim hats and peculiarity in dress. The two who traveled through our section always made it convenient to call at our house for dinner or a night's lodging. It was about the regular time for these gentlemen to come around, and near the dinner hour one of the servants came in announcing to mother that the Shakers were coming down the lane. This was a notice to increase the contents of the dinner pot.

THE BELL WITCH

The Witch spoke up immediately, exclaiming "Them damn Shakers shan't stop this time." Father was troubled a great deal by breachy stock on the outside pushing the fences down, and generally sent Harry, a negro boy, around every day to drive away stock and see that the fences were up.

There were three large dogs on the place that the boys always carried along, and he had them well trained and always eager for a chase, and would start at his call, yelping furiously. Harry was nowhere about. He was out on the farm with the other hands.

But instantly after the Witch spoke, Harry's voice was heard in the front yard calling the dogs, "Here, Caesar; here, Tige; here, Bulger, here, here, sic, sic," slapping his hands.

Not a soul but the Shakers coming down the lane could be seen. The dogs, however, responded with savage yelping, going in a fury, following the voice that led the way, urging them on, and just as the Shakers were nearing the turning-in gate, the dogs leaped the fence at their horses' heels, and Harry's voice was there, too, hollering, "Sic, sic, take 'em."

The Shakers put whip to their horses and the dogs after them, and the Witch vehemently urging the dogs on and hilariously enjoying the sport.

THE BELL WITCH

It was a lively chase, and broke the Shakers from coming that way again. The Witch enjoyed the sport greatly, laughing and repeating the affair to visitors, injecting many funny expressions in describing the chase, and how the Shakers held on to their big hats.

The story of the hazelnuts and grapes brought to mother during her illness was hard for many to believe, and it may prove a severe strain on the credulity of the reader, but it is nevertheless true, and will be verified by several worthy persons who witnessed the facts and have stated the same to many people.

The Witch had all along manifested a high regard for mother, often remarking, "Old Luce is a good woman."

This was very gratifying to the family; we were all much devoted to her, and this earnest expression of tender respect for her, so often repeated, was to a great extent an assurance that whatever might befall other members of the family, mother would be spared personal affliction. She was fearful of the thing, and could not see any good sense or policy in antagonizing what was now evidently a powerful, intelligent and incomprehensible agency, and therefore she conceived it to be the best policy to cultivate the kind manifestations of the Witch, as she did her ten-

THE BELL WITCH

der affections for her children. This proved to be the best policy, for it is evident that she appeased the seer's malice in many instances, except in fathr's case, toward whom the malignity was unrelenting and beyond control.

About the middle of September, 1820, mother was taken down with a spell of pleurisy, and then it was that the Witch manifested a sorrowful nature, growing more plaintive every day as the disease progressed, giving utterance to woeful expressions that were full of touching sympathy.

"Luce, poor Luce; I am so sorry you are sick. Don't you feel better, Luce? What can I do for you, Luce? These and many other expressions of sympathy and anxious inquiries were given vent by the saddened voice, that now appeared to remain constantly in mother's room, prattling all through the day, changing to a more joyful tone when she indicated any temporary relief. The persistent jabbering and disquietude was enough to craze a well person, but mother bore it all patiently, frequently replying to questions.

Sometimes she would reply, "Oh, I am too sick to talk to you."

Then the voice would hush for some time, as if choking expression. When anything was wanted or called for that was needed for mother's comfort, the Witch would speak promptly, telling pre-

THE BELL WITCH

cisely where the article could be found. And so the strange voice continued from day to day, mystifying every one who came to visit and minister to mother's wants, and it was utterly impossible to distinguish from whence it came, and yet so pathetic as to affect the sympathy of every one who came within hearing.

It was noticeable also that the Witch kept quiet when mother was apparently at rest, or sleeping. She rested better in the latter part of the night, and was somewhat refreshed for the morning, and as soon as she was aroused the Witch was heard inquiring, "How do you feel this morning, Luce? Did you rest well through the night? Don't you want to hear a song, Luce?"

Mother was very fond of vocal music, in which the Witch excelled, and it was her pleasure to reply, "Yes; sing something sweet."

While the Witch sang a number of beautiful stanzas, the following was the favorite, which was sung every day:

"Come, my heart, and let us try
    For a little season
Every burden to lay by.
    Come and let us reason.

THE BELL WITCH

What is this that casts you down?
    Who are those that grieve you?
Speak and let the worst be known.
    Speaking may relieve you.

Christ by faith I sometimes see,
    And He doth relieve me,
But my fears return again,
    These are they that grieve me.

Troubled like the restless sea,
    Feeble, faint and fearful,
Plagued with every sore disease,
    How can I be cheerful?"

No rhythmical sound or melody ever fell upon the ear with sweeter pathos, coming as it did like a volume of symphony from a bursting heart.

I have seen the tears trickle down mother's fevered cheeks while friends would turn away to hide repressed weeping. Sick as she was, mother never neglected to compliment the song. "Thank you; that was so sweet and beautiful. It makes me feel better," which the Witch seemed to appreciate.

Mother gradually grew worse, the disease reaching a serious stage. The doctor was still very hopeful, but the family and our good neigh-

THE BELL WITCH

bors were feeling the deepest concern. Father became very restless and apprehensive of the worst. Her appetite failed entirely, and this distressed the Witch very much. The neighbors brought all sorts of tempting good things to induce her to eat, and this example the observing Witch imitated, conceiving the idea, no doubt, that the most important thing was the discovery of something agreeable to her appetite, and this was the circumstance that seemed to have inspired the action of the Witch in bringing the nuts and grapes.

Wild fruits were plentiful in the woods about the place, and were then ripening. The first instance was the appearance of the hazelnuts. The same plaintive voice was heard exclaiming, "Luce, poor Luce, how do you feel now? Hold out your hands, Luce, and I will give you something."

Mother stretched her arms, holding her hands together open, and the hazelnuts were dropped from above into her hands. This was witnessed by several ladies who had called to see mother, and it was so incredible that the floor above was examined to see if there was not a loose plank or some kind of opening through which they were dropped, but it was found to be perfectly secure, and not even a crevice through which a pin could pass. After some time the amazement was in-

THE BELL WITCH

creased by the same voice inquiring, "Say, Luce, why don't you eat the hazlenuts?"

Mother replied that she could not crack them. Then the exclamation, "Well I will crack some for you," and instantly the sound of the cracking was heard, and the cracked nuts dropped on her bed within hand's reach, and the same passionate voice continued, insisting on mother's eating the nuts, that they would do her good. Next came the grapes in the same way, the voice importuning her to eat them, that they would do her good.

Mother was thoughtful in expressing her thanks, remarking, "You are so kind, but I am too sick to eat them."

From this on, mother steadily improved, coming out of a severe spell that held her down some twenty days, and no one could express more joy and gladness than the Witch, who also praised Dr. Hopson, the good physician who brought her through safely.

As soon as mother was convalescent, the Witch devoted more attention to the entertainment of the large number of visitors who were constantly coming to hear the mysterious voice.

One evening the room was full of company, all deeply interested in discussing the phenomena of the grapes, etc., when the presence of the Witch was announced by the voice exclaiming,

"Who wants some grapes?" and before any one could answer, a large bunch of luscious wild grapes fell upon Elizabeth's lap. The bunch was passed around and all tasted of the fruit, and were satisfied that it was no illusion.

The Witch evinced remarkable knowledge of the forest, and would tell us where to find plenty of grapes, hazelnuts, herbs of every kind, a good hickory for axe handles, or tough stick for a maul.

The Witch, as before intimated, visited the family of Brother Jesse Bell quite often, making demonstrations, but never to the extent of the manifestations at home.

Jesse's wife, whom the Witch called "Pots," observed mother's policy in humoring the Witch, paying kindly attention to its gabble, incurring favor or kindly relations, and she, too, was treated with such consideration as to relieve her fears of any immediate harm. Jesse Bell and Bennett Porter had determined to move with their families to Panola County, Mississippi, and were shaping their affairs to that end, as soon as circumstances would admit. This phenomena I give as related by Martha herself, there being no other witnesses to the circumstance, but I can not doubt her statement, which is borne out by other facts.

Late in the afternoon she was sitting outside

THE BELL WITCH

in the shade of the house, engaged in peeling apples for drying. She heard a kind of buzzing or indistinct whispering in her ear and recognized at once that it was the voice of the Witch, and spoke to it, inquiring, "What do you want? Speak out so I can understand you."

Then the Witch spoke plainly, saying, "Pots, I have brought you a present to keep in remembrance of me when you go to your far-away home. Will you accept it?"

She replied, "Certainly, I will gladly accept any present you may bring. What is it?"

Just then a small roll, neatly wrapped in paper, fell on her lap. She looked up and around in every direction, but no one was near, nor could she discover from whence it came.

In her confusion, the Witch spoke again, saying, "I brought it, Pots; see what a nice pair of stockings. I want you to keep them for your burial, to remember me, and never wear them."

She then stripped off the paper and found a pair of elegant black hose, for which she thanked the Witch, promising to keep them as requested. Martha said she discovered an ugly splotch on one of the hose, which she was eyeing with much curiosity, when the Witch spoke very promptly, remarking, "That is blood. They killed a beef at

THE BELL WITCH

Kate Batts' this morning and the blood spattered on the stocking."

Martha said she was so disconcerted and perplexed that she could not speak, and the Witch departed, or said nothing more. Jesse came in from the field very soon, and when made acquainted with all the facts as above stated, determined to go at once to the Batts' home and ascertain the facts regarding the Witch's story of the butchering that morning. He did not mention the circumstance, but very soon Mrs. Batts expressed herself as very glad that he had called, stating they had killed a fine young beef that morning, and intended sending Patsy (his wife) a piece, but had had no opportunity, and wished him to take it, which he did. So this part of the Witch's story was confirmed, and Jesse further ascertained from Mrs. Batts that it had been a very busy day, and not one of the family had left the place during that day, or, but for the pressing engagement, she would have sent the beef to his house. Moreover, Martha Bell had not left the premises, nor had any visitor been on the place.

During the period of these exciting demonstrations, ever so many detectives, wise men, witch doctors, or conjurors, came to exercise their skill on the Witch, and were permitted to practice schemes and magic arts to their hearts' content,

THE BELL WITCH

and all were brought to grief in some way, confessing that the phenomena was something beyond comprehension.

One notable instance was that of Dr. Mize of Simpson County, Kentucky, some thirty-five miles away, whose fame as a magician had been widely spread, and many brought word to father of his genius, urging him to send for the noted conjurer. The truth is, father had become alarmed about his own condition. His spells of contortions of the face, twitching of the flesh, and stiffness of the tongue, were gradually growing more frequent and severe.

His friends observed this and also that the animosity of the Witch toward him was increasing in vehemence, every word spoken to him being a blast of calumnious aspersions, and threatenings of some dire evil which was horrifying. He had also become convinced from his observations that this terrible thing had the power, as it claimed, to so afflict him, and that the purpose was to torture the life out of him, as it also declared; and under these circumstances he yielded to the many persuasions to exhaust all means and efforts to free himself and family from the tormentor.

He consulted with Mr. James Johnston about the matter, who thought it would be well to give

THE BELL WITCH

Dr. Mize a trial, and further proposed to go with Drew after the famous wizard. So it was agreed that Mr. Johnston and Drew were to start on the hunt for Dr. Mize after three o'clock in the morning, while the Witch was not about, and clear the neighborhood before the morning hour for the Witch's appearance. The whole matter was to be kept a profound secret, and no one was let into the understanding. Drew made ready to accompany Mr. Johnston on a business trip, to be absent two or three days, and that was all that was known about it.

They got off according to the arrangement in good time, and had perhaps passed Springfield before day.

The Witch came as usual that morning, observing first Drew's absence, setting up an anxious inquiry for him. Not one of the family could give any information concerning him, and the Witch seemed baffled and disappeared, and was not heard again during the day, but returned that night in great glee, having discovered the whole secret, telling all about Drew and Mr. Johnston's trip.

The Witch went on to say, "I got on their track and overtook them twenty miles on the way, and followed along some distance, and when I hopped in the road before them, looking like a

143

THE BELL WITCH

poor old sick rabbit, "Old Sugar Mouth" said, "There is your Witch, Drew; take her up in your lap. Don't you see how tired she is?"

The Witch continued to gossip about the trip in a hilarious way, manifesting much satisfaction in discovering the deep laid scheme, but no one knew how true the story was until Mr. Johnston and Drew returned the following evening, when they confirmed everything that the Witch had stated. Mr. Johnston said that he did not really believe at the time of calling Drew's attention to the rabbit that it was the Witch, but spoke of its peculiar action in a jocular way, as a mere matter of pastime, nor did Drew think otherwise of it.

They found Dr. Mize at his home east of Franklin, Ky., told him the story of our trouble, and the information received concerning his power to dispel witchery, etc. The Doctor said it was out of the ordinary line of phenomena, but he had no doubt of his ability to remove the spell and expose the craft that had brought it on, and he set the time, some ten days ahead, when he would be ready to begin the experiment.

Accordingly, the wise man put in his appearance, having studied the question, and was prepared for business, making boasts of his knowledge of spirits and skill in casting out devils, much

THE BELL WITCH

to the disgust of father, who had about sized him up on sight.

However, like others, Mize was treated courteously and allowed to pursue his own plans. The wizard stayed three or four days, hearing not a breath from the Witch. In the meantime, he found an old shotgun which had been out of repair some time, and he at once discovered that the Witch had put a spell on it. He soon cleaned the old gun, readjusted the lock and trigger, performed some conjurations, making the gun shoot as well as ever. This much, taken in consideration with the fact that the Witch had kept perfectly quiet since his arrival, he considered as remarkable progress, and he doubted the return of the Witch. Certain he was that the Witch would hardly show up as long as he remained; witches, he said, were always shy of him. So Mize continued, working sorcery, making curious mixtures, performing incantations, etc., to the amusement of those who observed his actions.

Finally, the Witch put in, questioning the con jurer impertinently as to what he was doing, and the object of his sorcery. Mize was nonplussed by the mysterious voice, which he had not before heard, recognizing that the Witch had come to keep company with him. He tried to be reticent and evasive, intimating that a witch had no busi-

THE BELL WITCH

ness prying into his affairs. The Witch, however, continued to ply him with hard questions, and finally suggested to Dr. Mize that he had omitted some very important ingredients for his charm mixture. "What is that?" inquired Mize, in astonishment.

"If you were a witch doctor you would know how to aerify that mess, so as to pass into the aeriform state, and see the spirit that talks to you, without asking silly questions," replied the Witch.

"What do you know about this business, anyhow?" again inquired the bewildered conjurer.

The Witch then told him that he was an old fool and didn't know what he was doing, and then let into cursing Mize like blue blazes. Such a string of blasting oaths was never heard, and Dr. Mize was frightened out of his wits, and was anxious to get away.

"That thing," he said, knew so much more about witchcraft than he did that he could do nothing with it. Mize arranged for an early start home the next morning. Somehow, the horse refused to go off kindly, rearing and kicking up. Finally, the Witch came to the rescue, proposing to make the horse go, and accompany the Doctor home. Immediately the horse started with a rush,

THE BELL WITCH

kicking and snorting, and went off at full speed, with the Doctor hanging on to the mane.

The Witch came that night in great glee, describing the trip home with the "old fraud," and the tricks played on him along the way, just as Mize described the affair to his neighbors.

Much has been talked about Bennett Porter shooting at the Witch. Porter, according to his own statement, did shoot at an object that appeared to his wife and Elizabeth, as described by them, but saw nothing himself except the bent saplings in motion.

This circumstance occurred during the time the witch family appeared on the scene. Elizabeth was there on a visit to her sister. Bennett Porter was absent during the day, filling an engagement at Fort's mill, which was in course of construction, and returned home late in the afternoon.

The hens were laying about the stables, which were located on the opposite side of the lane from the house. Esther started across the lane that afternoon to gather up the eggs. Just as she passed from the yard into the road, she observed a woman walking slowly up the lane toward the house, and she hurried on her mission and returned just in time to meet the lady at the front entrance. She recognized the person as one of

THE BELL WITCH

her neighbors, and spoke to her pleasantly, to which the woman made no reply. She repeated the salutation, which again failed to elicit any response. The woman appeared to have taken off her bonnet and let her hair down, and was engaged in combing out her hair as she walked, and stopped just opposite the house, where Esther met her, continuing the combing, and appeared deeply absorbed or troubled. Esther said she invited the lady in the house, repeating the solicitation several times, to which the woman paid no attention. She felt much chagrined by the strange conduct of her neighbor, and concluded that something was wrong with the lady or that she had become offended toward her, and she passed in, leaving the woman standing in the lane, combing her hair. She called Elizabeth's attention to the woman and her conduct, and they both observed her still in the same attitude. Presently, she climbed on the yard fence, and then she tucked it up in the usual way and left the fence, crossing over into the stable lot, where she could not possibly have had any business. The lot inclosed some three or four acres, a grove mostly of young saplings on the further side, in the midst of which was a large knotty log. The woman walked across the lot, passing around the log, when there appeared three other persons, two

THE BELL WITCH

younger women or girls, and a boy. Each one bent down a sapling, sitting upon them, riding up and down, giving motion to the spring afforded by the bush.

While this exercise still continued, Bennett Porter returned home, finding Esther and Elizabeth excited over the strange demonstrations, which they tried to point out to him. He said he could see the bushes in motion, but could not see the persons described. He suggested that they were the Witch apparitions, and got his gun, insisting that Esther should shoot at one of the objects. While he was getting his rifle, the appearances let the saplings up and took positions behind the log; Esther refused to shoot, but directed Porter to shoot near a large knot on the log where one of the heads appeared. He fired and his bullet cut the bark on the log just where he aimed, but nothing more was seen of the four persons, nor could they, as Porter thought, have escaped from the lot without detection. They all three went to the log and searched the lot over, but could discover no signs except the bent saplings and the mark of the bullet on the log.

Now, whether these were doubles, apparitions, witches or real persons, the witch family in their carousal that night made much ado about it, declaring to the company present that Bennett Porter had shot at Jerusalem and had broken his arm with the bullet.

I have written more about this abominable thing than contemplated in the outset, and still have not told the half, but have presented enough to which others can testify to enable the reader to form some idea of the heinous thing, and the horrors that our family had to endure during the early settlement of Robertson County, from an unknown enemy and for an unknown cause.

Whether it was witchery, such as afflicted people in past centuries and the darker ages, whether some gifted fiend of hellish nature, practicing sorcery for selfish enjoyment, or some more modern science akin to that of mesmerism, or some hobgoblin native to the wilds of the country, or a disembodied soul shut out from Heaven, or an evil spirit like those Paul drove out of the man into the swine, setting them mad; or a demon let loose from Hell, I am unable to decide; nor has any one yet divined its nature or cause for appearing, and I trust this description of the monster in all forms and shapes, and of many tongues, will lead experts who may come with a wiser generation to a correct conclusion and satisfactory explanation.

However, no part of what I have written would be complete without the finale; the climax which

THE BELL WITCH

I now approach with a shudder that fills my frame with horror, bringing fresh to memory scenes and events that chilled the blood in my young veins, cheating me out of twenty years of life. It hangs over me like the pall of death, and sends weary thoughts like fleeting shadows through my brain, reviving in memory those demoniac shrieks that came so oft from an invisible and mysterious source, rending the air with vile and hideous curses that drove me frantic with fear.

It is no ghastly dream of a fevered brain that comes to haunt one's thoughts, but a sad, fearful reality, a tremendous truth that thrills the heart with an unspeakable fear that no word painting can portray on paper.

Courageous men in battle line may rush upon bristling bayonets and blazing musketry, and face the roaring cannon's mouth, because they can see the enemy and know whom and what they are fighting; but when it comes to meeting an unknown enemy of demonstrative power, with gall upon its tongue and venom in its bosom, heaving bitter curses and breathing threatenings of dire consequences, which one knows not of, nor can judge in what shape or form the calamity is to come, the stoutest heart will prove a coward, faltering and quivering with painful fear.

THE BELL WITCH

Why should my father, John Bell, be inflicted with such a terrible curse? Why should such a fate befall a man striving to live uprightly?

I would be untrue to myself and my parentage should I fail to state boldly that John Bell was a man, every inch of him, and in every sense of the term. No man was ever more faithful and swift in the discharge of every duty, to his family, to the church, to his neighbors, to his fellow man, and to his God, in the fullness of his capacity, and that faith which led him to love and accept Christ as a Savior.

No mortal man ever brought a charge of delinquency or dishonor to his door. Not even the ghastly fiend that haunted him to his death, in all of its vile curses and evil threatenings, ever brought an accusation against him, or uttered a solitary word that reflected upon his honor, his character, his courage or his integrity.

He lived in peace and in the enjoyment of the full confidence of his neighbors, and lacked not for scores of friends in his severest trials.

Then why this infliction? Where the cause? Which no man, saint, angel from Heaven, or demon from Hell, has ever assigned. If there was any hidden or unknown cause why he should have thus suffered, or if it was in the providence of

THE BELL WITCH

God a natural consequence, then why should the torments of a demon have been visited upon Elizabeth, who was a girl of tender years, brought up under the careful training of a Christian mother and was free from guile and the wiles of the wicked world, and innocent of all offense?

Yet this vile, heinous, unknown devil, torturer of human flesh, that preyed upon the fears of people like a ravenous vulture, spared not her, but rather chose her as a shining mark for an exhibition of its wicked stratagem and devilish tortures. And never did it cease to practice upon her fears, insult her modesty, stick pins in her body, pinching and bruising her flesh, slapping her cheeks, disheveling and tangling her hair, tormenting her in many ways until she surrendered that most cherished hope which animates every young heart.

Was this the stratagem of a human genius skilled in the black art; was it enchantment, a freak of destiny, or the natural consequence of disobedience to some law in nature?

Let a wiser head than mine answer and explain the mystery.

Another problem in the development of these mysterious manifestations that has always puzzled my understanding: why should the husband and father, the head of the family, and the daughter, the pet and pride of the household, the center of all family affections, be selected to bear the invectives of this terrible visitation, while from the same source was bestowed upon the wife and mother demonstrations of the tenderest love?

If it was a living, intelligent creature, what could have been the dominating faculty of its nature, that made this discrimination? Could it have been an intelligent human devotion springing from an emotional nature that could so love the wife and mother, and cherish such bitter enmity for her husband and offspring, both of whom she loved most devotedly? Methinks not; only a fiend of a hellish nature with poisoned blood and seared conscience, if a conscience at all, could have possessed such attributes. Yet we, who experienced or witnessed the demonstrations, know that there was wonderful power of intelligence, possessing knowledge of men and things, a spirit of divination that could read minds, tell men's secrets, quote the Scriptures, repeat sermons sing hymns and songs, assume bodily forms, and withal, an immense physical force behind the manfestatons.

Father continued to suffer with spells as I have already described, the jerking and twitching of his face, and the swelling of his tongue, fearfully distorting his whole physiognomy.

THE BELL WITCH

These spells would last from one to two days, and after passing off, he would be up and about his business, apparently in strong, robust health. As time advanced the spells grew more frequent and severe, and there was no periodical time for their return, and along toward the last I stayed with him all the time, especially when he left the house, going with him wherever he went.

The Witch also grew more angry and virulent in disposition. Every word uttered to "Old Jack" was a blast of curses and heinous threats, while to mother, "Old Luce," it continued most tender, loving and kind.

About the middle of October father had a severe attack, which kept him confined to the house six or seven days. The Witch cursed and raved like a maniac for several days, and ceased not troubling him. However, he temporarily overcame this attack and was soon able to be out, though he would not venture far from the house. But it was not destined that he should enjoy a long respite. After a week's recuperation he felt much stronger, and called me very early one morning to go with him to the hog pen, some three hundred yards from the house, for the purpose of giving directions in separating the porkers intended for fattening from the stock hogs. We had not gone far before one of his shoes was

THE BELL WITCH

jerked off. I replaced it on his foot, drawing the strings tight, tying a double hard knot. After going a few steps farther the other shoe flew off in the same manner, which was replaced and tied as in the case of the first. In no way that I could tie them would they hold, notwithstanding his shoes fitted close and were a little hard to put on, and we were walking over a smooth, dry road. This worried him prodigiously; nevertheless, he bore up strongly, and after much delay and worry, we reached the place and he gave directions, seeing the hogs properly separated as he desired, and the hands left for other work, we started back for the house.

We had not gone many steps before his shoes commenced jerking off as before, and presently he complained of a blow on his face which felt like an open hand, that almost stunned him, and he sat down on a log that lay by the roadside. Then his face commenced jerking with fearful contortions. Soon his whole body; and then his shoes would fly off as fast as I could put them on.

The situation was trying and made me shudder. I was terrified by the spectacle of the contortions that seized father, as if to convert him into a very demon to swallow me up.

Having finished tying father's shoes, I raised

THE BELL WITCH

myself up to hear the reviling sound of derisive songs piercing the air with terrorizing force. As the demoniac shrieks died away in triumphant rejoicing, the spell passed off and I saw the tears chasing down father's yet quivering cheeks. The trace of faltering courage marked every lineament of his face with a wearied expression of fading hope. He turned to me with an expression of tender, compassionate, fatherly devotion, exclaiming in a woeful, passionate tone: "Oh, my son, my son, not long will you have a father to wait on so patiently. I cannot much longer survive the persecutions of this horrible thing. It is killing me by slow tortures, and I feel that the end is nigh." This expression sent a pang to my bosom which I had never felt before.

Mingled sorrow and terror took possession of me and sent a tremor through my frame that I can never forget. If the earth could have opened and swallowed us up, it would have been a joyful deliverance. My heart bleeds now at every pore as I pen these lines, refreshing my memory with thoughts of terror that possessed me then in anticipation of a fearful tragedy that might be enacted before father could move from his position.

That moment he turned his eyes upward and lifted his soul to heaven in a burst of fervent passionate prayer, such as I had never heard him utter before. He prayed the Lord that if it were possible to let this terrible affliction pass. He beseeched God to forsake him not in the trying ordeal, but to give him courage to meet this unknown devastating enemy in the trying emergency, and faith to lift him to the confidence and love of a blessed Saviour, and with all to relieve his family and loved ones from the terrible afflictions of this wicked, unknown, terrifying, blasphemous agency. It was in this strain that father prayed, pouring out his soul in a passionate force that afforded fresh courage and renewed strength. After he had finished his prayer, a feeling of calmness and reconciliation seemed to possess him, and he appeared to have recovered from the shock.

The reviling songster had disappeared and he rose up remarking that he felt better and believed he could walk to the house, and he did, meeting with no more annoyance as we proceeded on the way.

However, he took to his bed immediately on arrival at the house, and though able to be up and down for several weeks, he never left the house again, and seemed all the while perfectly reconciled to the terrible fate that awaited him. He gradually declined; nothing that friends could do

THE BELL WITCH

brought any relief. Mother was almost constantly at his bedside with all the devotion of her nature. Brother John attended closely in the room, ministering to him, and good neighbors were constant in attendance. The Witch was carrying on its deviltry more or less all the time.

The crisis, however, came on the morning of December 19th. Father, sick as he was, had not up to this time failed to awake at his regular hour, according to his long custom, and arouse the family. That morning he appeared to be sleeping so soundly, mother quietly slipped out of the room to superintend breakfast, while brothers John and Drew looked after the farm hands and feeding the stock, and would not allow him to be disturbed until after breakfast. Noticing then that he was sleeping unnaturally, it was though best to awaken him, when it was discovered that he was in a deep stupor, and could not be aroused to any sensibility.

Brother John attended to giving him medicine, and went immediately to the cupboard where he had carefully put away the medicines prescribed for him, but instead he found a smoky looking vial, which was about one-third full of dark-colored liquid.

He set up an inquiry at once to know who had moved the medicine, and no one had touched it,

THE BELL WITCH

and neither could any one on the place give an account of the vial.

Dr. George Hopson of Port Royal was sent for in great haste, and soon arrived; also neighbors John Johnston, Alex. Gunn, and Frank Miles arrived early and were there when the vial was found.

The Witch in the meantime broke out with joyous exultation, exclaiming: "It's useless for you to try to relieve Old Jack—I have got him this time; he will never get up from that bed again."

The Witch was then asked about the vial of medicine found in the cupboard, and replied: "I put it there, and gave Old Jack a big dose out of it last night while he was fast asleep, which fixed him."

This was all the information that could be drawn from the Witch or any other source concerning the vial of medicine. Certain it was that no member of the family ever saw it before, or could tell anything about it. In fact, no vial and no medicine of any kind had been brought to the house by any one else except by Dr. Hopson, and then it was handled carefully. Dr. Hopson, on arrival, examined the vial and said he did not leave it and could not tell what it contained. It

THE BELL WITCH

was then suggested that the contents be tested on something.

Alex. Gunn caught a cat, and brother John ran a straw into the vial and drew it through the cat's mouth, wiping the straw on its tongue. The cat jumped and whirled over a few times, stretched out, kicked and died in a short while.

Father lay all day and night in a deep stupor, as if under the influence of some opiate, and could not be aroused to take any medicine. The Doctor said he could detect something on his breath that smelled very much like the contents of the vial which he had examined. How father could have gotten it was a mystery that could not be explained in any other way except that testified by the Witch. The vial and contents were thrown into the fire, and instantly a blue blaze shot up the chimney like a flash of powder.

Father never revived or returned to consciousness for a single moment. He lingered along through the day and night, gradually wearing away, and on the morning of December 20, 1820, breathed his last.

The Witch was around during the time, indulging in wild exultations and derisive songs. After father breathed his last, nothing more was heard from the Witch until after the burial was completed. It was a bright December day and a great

THE BELL WITCH

crowd of people came to attend the funeral. Rev. Suggs Fort and Revs. James and Thomas Gunn conducted the services. After the grave was filled and the friends turned to leave the sad scene the Witch broke out in a loud voice, singing, "Row me up some brandy, O," and continued singing this until the family and friends had all entered the house. And thus ended one Chapter in the series of exciting and frightful events that kept the whole neighborhood so long in a frenzy and worked upon our fears from day to day.

After the death of John Bell Sr., the fury of the Witch was greatly abated. There were but two purposes, seemingly, developed in the visitation. One was the persecution of father to the end of his life. The other, the vile purpose of destroying the anticipated happiness that thrilled the heart of Betsy. This latter purpose, however, was not so openly manifested as the first, and was of such a delicate nature that it was kept a secret as much as possible in the family, and ignored when talked about, but it never ceased its tormenting her until her young dream was destroyed.

The Witch remained with us after father's death through the Winter and Spring of 1821, all the while diminishing or becoming less demonstrative. Finally, it took leave of the family, bid-

THE BELL WITCH

ding mother, "Luce," an affectionate farewell, saying that it would be absent seven years, but would return to see us and would then visit every house in the neighborhood.

This promise was fulfilled as regards the old homestead, but I do not know that it visited other homes in the vicinity. It returned during February, 1828. The family was then nearly broken up. Mother, Joel and I were the only occupants left at the old homestead, the other members of the family having settled off to themselves.

The demonstrations announcing its return were precisely the same that characterized its first appearance. Joel occupied a bed in mother's room and I slept in another apartment alone. After considerable scratching on the weatherboarding on the outside, it appeared in the same way on the inside, scratching on the bedpost and pulling the cover from my bed as fast as I could replace it, keeping me up nearly all night.

It went on in this way for several nights, and I spoke not a word about it, lest I should frighten mother. However, one night later, after worrying me for some time, I heard a noise in mother's room and knew at once what was to pay. Very soon mother and Joel came rushing into my room, much frightened, telling me about the disturbance and something pulling the cover off. We sat up

THE BELL WITCH

till a late hour discussing the matter, satisfied that it was the same Witch, and agreed not to talk to the Witch, and that we would keep the matter a profound secret to ourselves, worrying with it the best we could, hoping that it would leave as it did after disturbing us in this way some two weeks, and this was my last experience with it.

The Witch came and went, hundreds of people witnessed its wonderful demonstrations, and many of the best people of Robertson and adjoining counties have testified to these facts, telling the story over and over to the younger generation, and for this and other reasons, as before stated, I have written this much of the details as correctly as it is possible to state the exciting events.

So far, no one has ever given any intelligent or comprehensive explanation of the great mystery. Those who came as experts were worse confounded than all others.

As I before stated, a few mendacious calumniators were mean enough to charge that it was tricks and inventions of the Bell family to make money, and I write for the purpose of branding this version as an infamous falsehood. It was well known in the vicinity and all over the county that every investigation confirmed the fact that the Bell family were the greatest, if not the only sufferers from the visitation, and that no one or

THE BELL WITCH

a dozen persons in collusion could have so long, regularly and persistently practiced such a fraud without detection, nor could they have known the minds and secrets of strangers visiting the place and detailed events that were then occurring or had just transpired in different localities. Moreover, the visitation entailed great sacrifice.

As to how long this palavering phenomenon continued in the vicinity, I am unable to state. It did not disturb the remaining members of the family at the old place any more.

Mother died shortly after this and the house was entirely deserted, the land and other property being divided among the heirs. The old house stood for some years, and was used for storing grain and other farm products, and was finally torn down and moved away.

Many persons professed to have seen sights and heard strange sounds about the old house and in the vicinity, all along up to this day. Several have described to me flitting lights along the old lane and through the farm, while others profess to have heard sounds of wonderfully sweet music and strange voices uttering indistinct words. And it is said that such things have been seen and heard at various places in the neighborhood, but I have no personal knowledge of the facts.

CHAPTER VII

JOHN BELL JR.'S RECOLLECTIONS OF THE SPIRIT

John Bell Jr., was born in North Carolina in 1793, several years before his father, John Bell, Sr., emigrated to Tennessee; however, his real boyhood days were in Tennessee. He spent his early days on his father's farm and learned how to farm and do all the things boys did on the farm at that time; his specialty was shooting a rifle. He could hit a turkey's head at one hundred yards as often as he tried, and could "bark" a squirrel from the tallest trees—that is, shoot between the squirrel and the limb it was on, knocking it out without wounding it.

When not quite eighteen years of age, he happened to be at Springfield one day where he saw an officer recruiting for the army. He immediately walked home to get his father's permission to enter the service, which was readily given, and he became a soldier. He served through the Indian campaigns, and was with General Jackson at New Orleans when he defeated the British.

After the war he, his brother Drewry, and Alexander Porter took up flatboating, taking the

THE BELL WITCH

products of their neighborhood, which consisted of smoked meats, lard, maple syrup, flour, tobacco and many other products, to New Orleans. They made these trips two or three times a year, making what was considered at that time good money. While on these trips, John Jr., came in contact with men in New Orleans who spoke French. He soon learned to speak this language fairly well.

He became the owner of one of the largest and best farms in Robertson County. He married Elizabeth Gunn, daughter of Rev. Thomas Gunn, in 1828. When the Spirit made its return visit, he was living at his own home, having established this home before his marriage. He owned many slaves and acquired what at that time was a fortune.

He was against secession, so voting, which did not add to his popularity. Having been a soldier, his services were very much needed, and when so solicited, he would get out a map of the United States and show his friends that the South could not defeat the North. He said they did not have the men; that the North had the money and seacoast, and that it took money to carry on war.

When told that one Southerner could whip five Yankees, he would reply, "That is true now, but

THE BELL WITCH

can't be done over a period of years; the Yankees will become trained soldiers after a few years." None of his neighbors believed the war would last "a few years."

After seeing the suffering and real war going on for a year, he determined that he must enter and do what he could for his beloved South, although at an advanced age. Before he could follow his determination to enter the war, he was suddenly seized with pneumonia, and died May 8th, 1862.

He was a man of indomitable courage and striking appearance, six feet three inches tall, and weighed one hundred and ninety pounds. It was said that he was a perfect image of his father. He was of a most dignified manner, but too stern looking to attract the average man. No one who knew him ever doubted his absolute honesty and truthfulness. He was considered a man of great intellect, and his reasoning powers were of the profoundest character.

Dr. J. T. Bell related that his father certainly went through an ordeal, witnessing the Spirit's cruel treatment of his father, which would have crazed the average man; and he had not a doubt that a day never passed that the sufferings and tragic death of his father did not pass before his eyes, causing him bitter thoughts which were never expressed, and gave to those who knew him the false impression that he was a man too stern and unrelenting for ordinary men to approach. He was always ready to lend money to his neighbors, no mortgage ever being taken.

He knew more than any other person of the Spirit, but had less to say about it than any one. He knew that his brother, Richad Williams, had written recollections of it, but he did not discuss what he himself knew, after the Spirit left. When the Spirit first appeared, he was nearly twenty-four fears of age and about twenty-eight when it left. When it returned after an absence of seven years, he was at the height of his intellectual powers, and during its first visit he was of an age to deliberate over these demonstrations in an intelligent manner. His natural good sense and courage enabled him to form opinions far better than the ordinary person.

His personal appearance and reputation were such that no one unhesitatingly brought up the subject of the Spirit in his presence. His son's wife, Mrs. J. T. Bell, related that one time she had asked his opinion of the Spirit, but he gave her no real answer and she could not form an opinion of what he thought. Never at any time did she hear him say anything of it.

Dr. J. T. Bell said he never heard his father

THE BELL WITCH

speak of the Spirit but three times. He gave him then his recollections which he took about three days to relate; he gave recollections of his own personal knowledge, of events occurring during the Spirit's stay on its first visit, an account of his father's death, and of the Spirit's departure soon after. He also gave a full account of his conferences with the Spirit on its return visit. No one but J. T. Bell and Frank Miles ever knew of its visit to John Bell Jr.'s on this last visitation; as stated elsewhere, he did not wish to excite the other members of the family, and soon knew the Spirit did not expect him to tell of its conferences with him.

Frank Miles was present at its farewell, and John Jr., told no one but his son, J. T. Bell.

He had the deepest respect and great confidence in Frank Miles, and when he told him to say nothing of the return visit of the Spirit, that was sufficient; their friendship was absolutely of the most binding character; their fidelity toward each other was unsurpassed.

John Jr., began studying the Spirit's actions seriously when it punished his sister Betsy without cause. He saw the marks left on Betsy's face and heard some of the mean words spoken to her; it did not talk to her in his presence as much or so severely as it did when he was absent. He heard the warnings given, "Not to marry Joshua Gardner."

On one occasion, after Betsy had gone to a neighbor's, the Spirit reappeared and said, "John, Betsy must not marry Joshua; see to it that she does not."

John asked the Spirit why it acted so vile. He said he would not do as it asked, and wanted to know just why Betsy should not marry Jushua, when she became old enough.

The Spirit replied, "If she marries Joshua, she can never have a day of happiness or peace; that is certain. That is the only reason I will give you, and if you cannot see that it is a good one, it is because of your stubbornness and not lack of sense. Betsy will take your advice; she knows that you idolize her and that your advice would be the best for her."

John replied, "I noticed the seemingly invisible threat 'that she will never have a happy day if she marries Joshua Gardner.' Do you want me to know that you would be the factor causing her unhappiness, as you have done so long?"

The Spirit said, "You may form your own conclusions, for I shall not answer that question, but once for all, Betsy would do better not to marry him, regardless of anything I may do. Future generations will prove it to be so."

THE BELL WITCH

After John Bell's death, Betsy and other members of the family thought for a short while that the Spirit had relented, and she was almost persuaded to marry Joshua when the Spirit again appeared and strongly urged her not to marry him. It again had a conference with John Jr., and almost demanded that he stop this marriage. John asked why the Spirit should be so absolute in its wishes to be obeyed in the matter of Betsy's marriage. There was never a real reply to this. John at all times said there was no reason in such a demand, but having that which was best for Betsy in mind, had a talk with her. Neither he nor she divulged what they had to say, but J. T. Bell had reasons to believe his father told Betsy that, in his opinion, in view of his father's fate, she would be asuming a great risk to marry Joshua. The same day of their discussion Betsy, with great reluctance, told Joshua of her decision not to marry him. That John Jr. approved of her decision there could scarcely be a doubt.

John Jr., advised his brother Drewry to marry. Drewry led a very lonely, apprehensive life, always fearing the Spirit would return.

It had given Drewry severe punishment. John Jr., said that on one occasion Drewry was leaning against a large, heavy bureau, which would have taken two men to move it, when the Spirit suddenly jerked it away from him, giving him a severe fall, bruising his face and otherwise hurting him. Drewry laboring under the nervous strain from his remembrances of the Spirit's actions, decided never to marry. He constantly thought of the terrible scenes through which he had passed. He died in 1865.

John Jr., did not deign to even speak of foolish persons thinking that some member of the Bell family was causing these demonstrations; he knew of some saying that he and Drewry could have learned some "magic arts" in New Orleans, and were showing their gifts at home, but he knew they would soon learn of their mistake when he and Drewry were not there.

Some people accused Betsy of ventriloquism; John Jr., suggested to a doctor who was visiting there from a distant state that he satisfy himself as to whether Betsy's voice could be used so. The doctor placed his hand over Betsy's mouth at the time the voice was heard, and soon satisfied himself that she was in no way connected with these sounds.

John Jr., only pointed with ridicule to any idea that Betsy or any member of the family, or any **person** could sing with the voice with which the Spirit was almost daily astonishing them.

He did not fail to notice, as every one else had,

THE BELL WITCH

that his mother, called "Luce," in an affectionate manner by the Spirit, had influence over the Spirit, which at all times kept her from personal harm. He could not understand why there was such a difference in the Spirit's treatment of his mother and sister; therefore in his first personal conference with the Spirit, he did not just ask, but demanded why it could not treat his sister and father as considerately as it did his mother. He told the Spirit a demon of the vilest character should be ashamed to have itself spoken of for all times as the most cruel, unjust being ever to have visited this earth; he taunted the Spirit with being a coward for persecuting a young innocent girl, and taking advantage of its unseen powers.

He invited the Spirit to inflict this punishment on him instead of his sister, telling it sternly, "you are a cowardly being of whom I have no fear, and I tell you again, destroy me, but if you think I care, then you will get no pleasure from your performance. My time on earth will be of short duration. When I leave here I have hopes of a better existence; as to you, I am sure you are doomed to an everlasting condition of unhappiness. Your actions could not give pleasure to the devil himself."

The Spirit replied to this, "John, I admit it is beyond my knowledge why I do not give you pun-

THE BELL WITCH

ishment for what you say; somehow your daring me to do as I like, no matter what you say, gives me respect for you, and I shall not favor you by punishing you, instead of Betsy. I know you and am convinced that I would give you pleasure to change her punishment to you. There are reasons why I will not punish you both; there are many things I want to say to some human being with enough intelligence to understand; even a monster as you think me when doomed to inhabit your world for a time would like to talk to a soul who is not so frightened and has so little sense it could not understand the things I say. You are correct; I am not getting happiness in your world. I have no such thing, nor have I ever had. I do not deny my hope for a day of happiness passed hundreds of years ago. Now, John, don't you think when such a being does anything at all which you might call good, no matter how insignificant, that a human being who is of the Spirit that the Creator of all things wishes would feel more kindly toward that being? Your mother is such a human. She is protected from all wickedness by her goodness and gentleness toward every creature of whatsoever kind, and always appreciative of the smallest tribute rendered her, even when extended to her by a demon."

John Jr., said, "The only virtue I have known

THE BELL WITCH

you to have, other than kindness to my mother, is that you do not deny being just as mean as you are. I sometimes think you are here because you so far excelled the demons of your world that they cast you out. I have wondered if demon Spirits really have fights with each other."

The Spirit replied, "John, I partially agree with you. I must remind you of another virtue. With you and "Luce" I have been absolutely truthful. You will never know of me telling you or your mother a lie. It may be you will not be able to understand all that I say to you, but remember, John, it will be true. The things I have told others which were not true were not important, but were told to prove how foolish the average human being really is. The man who can be easiest shown up to be a fool is ever ready to display his lack of sense over and over again. You must agree with me that a demon is not the only being who at times laughs at foolish things men do and encourages them to continue their foolish acts."

Several months previous to this conversation John Jr., had decided to make a trip to North Carolina to see after an estate which his father was interested in, and from which he was expecting considerable money. The Spirit broke into the family conference regarding this trip to tell John that no such estate had been wound up, and

THE BELL WITCH

that he was about to start out on a foolish trip, assuring him he would do better to remain at home.

John Jr., stated to J. T. Bell that the Spirit talked to him on his long horseback journey, assuring him that he was now determined to go on because he did not wish to be influenced by what had been told him. John Jr., was gone several months, and did not get a penny; many things occurred at home while he was away which he would have enjoyed more than the tiresome journey. He stated that the Spirit did not at any time laugh at him or say anything further about it being a foolish trip, but kept him informed of occurrences at home, and on his return his mother told him it had told her each day while he was on his journey of his progress, not neglecting to say, "John is stubborn, not just foolish; this is the way of human beings."

John Jr., then told that the Spirit's continued cruel treatment of his father had caused him repeated spells of illness, which kept growing worse. In his conferences with the Spirit it would not say anything of any connection it may have had with this illness, nor would it promise to quit its cruel treatment of his father, steadfastly refusing to give any other reason than that some day some generation would benefit by it.

THE BELL WITCH

It told him that when his father had these attacks his fortitude and great patience in bearing them without breaking his trust in God was enough to again prove that no matter if it did intend the death of John Bell finally, many men had died a worse death whose passing was known to benefit the world, nor did it preclude the final good result on account of their tormentors being sinful creatures, but to the contrary. There was no denying that his father was a man of unexcelled fortitude, and that he could not go through it all, nor could any man, without spiritual aid. It told him to make his conclusions from this.

"I see no reason whatever in your talk," John replied. "If my father were being punished on account of being wrong in his views of worship, or if he were denounced as a hypocrite, or a great sinner, then I might think of some creature who could think he should be punished; but even you cannot see anything, that you will tell, which would give any excuse for your heinous conduct toward my father. As long as you insist on talking to me, if it were till the end of the world, I shall say you need not tell me of the future good it all may do. I neither believe you nor want to hear it."

"Now, John," said the Spirit, "I will not take the advantage of you that I can and punish you

THE BELL WITCH

on account of your talk. I think better of you for it, and some day when your wrath is cooled I will try to tell you of things more pleasant, au plaisir de vous revoir (till I have the pleasure of seeing you again, adieu)." The Spirit spoke all languages fluently.

He related that the Spirit never at any time talked against Christianity, but always displayed great knowledge in its admonitions that the world did not think enough of the great sacrifices Christians had made for the future welfare of mankind. While at times the Spirit talked in a blasphemous tirade, using the most wicked phrases, it never ceased repeating that it mattered not how intelligent a man seemed, if he did not recognize the divinity of Jesus Christ, then he is not in accord with the greatest minds of the world. It told him to pass down to his posterity that never at any time had it wished any human being to have doubts of the existence of the Almighty Creator of all things, and while despairing of ever having a happy day, believing its present plight was for all eternity, that if ever summoned before the Great Being, it would be known it had never at any time resented His rule of the Universe.

"It is useless for you to try to make out your case to me," replied John Jr., "I am already prejudiced against you. I do not believe Jesus Christ

THE BELL WITCH

appreciates your defense of his Divinity. Why should he? You have not influenced and do not know the great Christians of the world. (John advised in his recollections that he was attempting to lead the Spirit to tell him of such observations it had made, and it will be noted that his adroitness was productive of results.)

The Spirit replied, "You are correct, in a way; my influence would not produce great results. I am an admitted outcast, but you are quite wrong when you say that I do not know the great Christians of this world. I have seen the great things they have accomplished, and know the minds of some of the world's greatest people who bow to the Christian religion. Certainly I could do no good, as you state, but I can inform you of what great thinkers conclude. Napoleon, possessed of the greatest mind on earth, has repeatedly recognized the Eternal future as taught by Jesus Christ. When his great friend Marshal Duroc was dying on the battlefield, he told him they would meet again in another life; this was not the end. He has said that he wants to die a Christian; dying slowly on the rocks of St. Helena, suffering from the almost unbearable climate, and no hope of either living much longer or escaping, he has said that his empire was founded by armies and the kingdoms of most of the great rulers of the past had been so founded; that while he was present soldiers followed him and would cheerfully die at his command, but now that he was gone he no longer had the love of his former followers, his empire was gone and he thought all the great earthly rulers had to be present to sustain their kingdoms. Jesus Christ would never be forgotten; his kingdom was founded on love and after centuries it is stronger now than at any time, and this without a doubt proved to him that Jesus Christ was God."

John, do not let the world forget that Napoleon's downfall was caused by forgetting that God's laws were still in force; that he thought only of himself; his ambition was unquenchable; had he stopped at the time which would have been best for France and the whole of Europe, he would have been acting for the everlasting good of mankind. He is mortal, therefore forgot God until trouble came; then, like a real man with a soul, acknowledged the Divinity of Jesus Christ, and we clearly see that he repented and will die quietly resigned to that fate, to which all human beings must bow. The world will never forget Napoleon, but the greatest thing he ever did they will not know or hear of—his acknowledgement of the Divinity of Jesus Christ, that he himself was

THE BELL WITCH

only a human; that his downfall was the result of a selfish foundation of his empire by force.

After the fall of Napoleon, the leading allied powers formed the Holy Alliance, taking the New Testament as their guide. They proposed to rule according to the Christian religion, love and justice being their aspiration. If these sovereigns were sincere the world would be safe. They are human and looking after their personal political interest, always leaning toward despotism. In time their governments will fall. These sovereigns are professing to believe in the Christian religion, but applying it in a way to suit their personal interests. This is the foundation for a great world disaster. They are not thinking of the welfare of their subjects, but really have formed an alliance for sovereigns to hold their subjects under tyrannical subjection if they wish. There is unrest and revolution in Europe and will be continued dissatisfaction until the final upheaval caused by sovereigns entirely forgetting their professed allegiance to Christianity; seeking only to satisfy their ambition. I have witnessed the things I am telling you, and am sure the final penalty will be terrible."

"In your country, John, you have a President who is earnestly looking after the welfare of his fellow citizens. He desires protection of the Uni-

THE BELL WITCH

ted States from European aggression. Before his administration is over his endeavors will place the Americas in a position of security. President Monroe is a man of honesty, whose administration is giving the people a realization of what may be accomplished rapidly in this country in every line, while not assuming great Christianity, the people are his first thought and his actions are that of a Christian. Jefferson's esteem for his goodness is as great as a man can have for another. Monroe's contact with Jefferson has been of great value to him and the nation. You remember Jefferson was the author of the statute of Virginia for religious freedom; he still lives and you know what he thinks of Christianity."

John Jr., related that after the long-continued punishment, loss of sleep, and uncertainty as to what would be meted out to him next, his father's nervous symptoms became greater.

On the morning of October 20, 1820, John Bell and his son, Richard Williams, walked to the hog pens, which were several hundred yards from the house. They both told on their return of the terrible punishment John Bell received. (This is related in Richard Williams' manuscript.)

John Jr., said, "On their return to the house I helped my father to bed; his shoe strings were broken, his feet had bleeding gashes on them; his

THE BELL WITCH

face was livid in spots as from blows; his eyes were red and watery, as though he had received punches in both eyes; his face was contorted and twitching; he still complained of pain all over his face, in his eyes and about his head. Richard Williams was so excited he was almost incoherent; as soon as he could, he told of the terrible punishment given father; it had ceased before they had arrived at the house. For some reason the Spirit never gave father the cruel treatment in the presence of mother and me as it did when neither of us were present.

Although knowing it to be useless, I at once went outside and invited the Spirit back, so enraged that for the first time since I had become a man I lost all reasoning power and implored God to send back this demon and give me for once some chance to return the same cruel punishment to it that it had given to father. I knew that as a man, unaided by divine power, I could not cope with this demon. I begged for this aid on my knees. I pleaded with God to send it back at once, but there was no return of it at that time.

My son, I tell you that which I have never told any human before and never shall again, I felt in my heart and spoke aloud out there in my father's yard, "My God, if thou art a just God, why allow this horrible punishment to a just man who has not offended?" My son, I have doubted Hell as generally accepted since that time; it must be here on earth. Neither can I understand God's ways. I know Christians have suffered and died, but I know of none but father, except Job, who ever suffered without knowing any cause; nor do I believe there ever was a real Job. I can not conceive of Almighty God punishing a good man for the purpose of proving to the devil that he would be good in spite of adversity. After that day my mother and I were constantly with father, trying to comfort him and possibly by our presence lessen the punishment he would receive at the hands of the Spirit.

My father was never able to be out again. He was in bed a few days, getting up, then having to take to his bed again, suffering from the attacks of pain about his face and head, and exhibiting the nervous twitching about his mouth. The Spirit at times taunted him in an exulting way. Father kept quiet and seemed resigned to his fate, the Spirit telling him each day he would die; that it was causing his death.

Drewry and I spent all of our time with father; I gave him medicines which the doctor left. Nearly every dose given, the Spirit would say, "That is of no use; I am going to kill him."

It would be difficult to imagine the ordeal

through which father was passing, suffering so intensely, and knowing his fate eventually was to be certain death. While father was sick this last time he did not give up waking early and arousing the family.

On the morning of December 19, Drewry and I went out early as usual to look after feeding the stock. On our return to father we found him unconscious. I was not surprised. He had not expected to recover and neither did we believe the Spirit would allow him a respite. We sent for his physician, Dr. George Hopson, who arrived within less than two hours. John Johnston, Alex Gunn and Frank Miles arrived very quickly. I spent some time attempting to arouse him, but failed to do so. I went to the cupboard where the bottles of medicine were kept; however, I did not believe it possible that he could swallow it if I'd known which to give, which I did not, for he had not been in such a condition before. I thought he was dying. The three bottles of medicine which I had been giving him were gone, and in their place was a dark bottle containing a brown fluid which none of us had ever seen before. Frank Miles, John Johnston and Alex Gunn each looked at it.

Frank had seen all the medicines we had given and he at once said, "The damned Witch did this."

THE BELL WITCH

The Spirit called out with great glee, "He will never get up. I did it."

It said it had given father a dose from the vial which would cause his death, but that was all we could get the Spirit to say regarding the vial. Frank Miles swore, prayed and did everything he could to provoke a quarrel with the Spirit to cause it to say where the vial came from, but never a word could he get it to say.

Dr. Hopson was the only person bringing any medicine to the house; when he arrived he at once said he knew nothing of this vial and did not know what it contained. He suggested that its contents be tested on a cat. Alex Gunn caught a cat, then I dipped a straw into the bottle, getting a small amount of its contents; while Alex held the cat's mouth open I wiped the straw off in its mouth. The cat soon began having convulsions and died within a few hours. I then threw the bottle into the fire. No one has ever known the contents of the vial.

Father never regained consciousness. He was never able to swallow any more medicine. We could only wait for the end, which came on the morning of December 20, 1820. The Spirit talked as if it enjoyed the scene of father's death. It laughed and sang and told us it would be at the funeral; then it quit talking.

THE BELL WITCH

After the funeral services, while the grave was being filled, the Spirit began singing wild songs in the presence of as large a concourse of people as ever attended a burial service in our country.

The Spirit was not at our home so often after father's death, and its demonstrations were milder. After Betsy's determination not to marry Joshua Gardner, it even attempted to talk nicely to her, but Betsy always remained silent. It commended her for her good judgment in giving up Joshua and would attempt to cheer her up. It remained till late in the Spring of 1821, coming to our home less frequently each week, saying very little to me, and seemingly avoided coming when I was at the house. I thought this was caused by its knowledge of my utter detestation of it and that my father's death had greatly intensied that feeling."

Some time after the death of John Bell, a beautiful snow covered the ground some eight or ten inches deep. During one of John Jr.'s conferences with the Spirit at that time, he upbraided the Spirit for causing his father's death. During the course of which he told the Spirit that his father's untimely death was doubly cruel, in that there was absolutely no cause for it, and he was removed from a family who so loved him, while yet with many years before him. Now they would

THE BELL WITCH

see their father no more, neither would he have the great pleasure and happiness of seeing his children's prosperity, being cut off in the cruel manner that he had been.

The Spirit said, "John, your father sees each day what his children are doing, and is now at peace with the prospect of seeing your future happiness."

"I can never be completely happy," John said, "when I feel each day the horror of having had to look upon my dying father for the last time, killed in such a manner and knowing of his love and pride in me, and he not to know of any of the good things I may possibly do."

"John, if your father could speak to you, he would tell you of his satisfaction. I could imitate his voice so you would not know but what it was his, but it is not my purpose to deceive you. I know you would not believe it to be really your father speaking. People who have gone on, whose souls have left their bodies, do not at this era talk to those left behind. Such a time, I tell you, will not likely ever be. Think of the uproar and constant excitement that would be created by such a condition! There is enough talking going on in the world now without the souls of thousands of years having a say. It is well understood that a human dreams and feels so sure it was real, that occasionally he feels as though he had communicated with a departed one; but that dreamer still has the most impressive recollection of things said and done by perhaps a loved one, and while in a condition to dream there passes through his brain the very things that he would like to know, sometimes things he preferred would not come to pass. More often, John, you know a dream amounts to nothing."

John asked the Spirit, "Why do you predict that a time must come when the Spiritual attitude of the world must change? If one has no way of knowing anything of what has gone before, how can human beings be encouraged to keep up good for evil?"

The Spirit answered, "You must know, as I have said to you before, there are so many things that are beyond the grasp of the human mind that faith in unknown power must be their salvation; that unknown power can not be understood; accept it through faith."

"You talk good when you like," John replied, "and always have, but act quite differently; understand me once again, I can not feel otherwise than I do toward you; such a being as you are, I presume, can not do otherwise than you have done. You would not be what you are if you could have prevented it. My father has said as

THE BELL WITCH

much to me. He only asked for strength from his Maker to bear the sufferings inflicted upon him, and did not direct supplications to you."

The Spirit said, "Your father is beyond all my power or any other except the Almighty Creator's. He is not of this world and it is not good that we talk further of him. I have told you that I might disturb and cause some doubts in your mind by doing things that would appear to be your father. I have no desire, as I repeatedly tell you, to deceive you. Now, mark this, you see no tracks in the snow leading to your window (John looked and there were no tracks); now observe tracks being made approaching your window."

Within a few moments the snow was disturbed as if some one were walking in it, and came directly to the window from which John Jr., was looking out. The tracks seemed to be made from heavy boots.

The Spirit now said, "If you have any doubts that I could have deceived you, or had you worried, take your father's old boots from the back porch and see if they fit those tracks."

John declined to do this.

The Spirit then reiterated, "I did that, and tell you that it was to prove I will not at any time deceive you on any subject we may be discussing. Your father could not make tracks here, or do

THE BELL WITCH

anything else that some foolish people might think or say. When I bid you and your folks good-bye, I shall not be seen or heard here again until I show what I am doing on my return. Do not ever worry about me being here until that time. I shall not worry you or your people when I make my next visit to you."

John related, "The Spirit made its final visit, bidding us all good-bye, one evening as we were all sitting around the fire after our evening meal. A ball something like a cannon ball rolled down the chimney and out into the room, bursting like a smoke ball.

A voice clearly called out, "I am going, and will be gone seven years. Good-bye to all."

We all felt greatly relieved, but I must say that we dreaded the promised visit for the next seven years.

Never at any time did I doubt the return of the Spirit; neither did my mother and Drewry; the other members were rather skeptical about it. Drewry spent the rest of his life expecting it back any day, regardless of its promise. The entire neighborhood also felt very much relieved.

For several years we had many visitors from distant parts of the country who had either not heard of its departure or through curiosity wished to see the place and meet us. To these visitors

THE BELL WITCH

I have always been courteous, but said nothing of the Spirit that would have been of interest to any one."

(The author will add that at the present time, one hundred and six years after the Spirit's last departure, an occasional visitor appears at the old place, and they always say "they just wanted to be able to say they had seen the place made so famous by what they called the "Bell Witch.")

CHAPTER VIII

JOHN BELL JR.'S RECOLLECTIONS OF THE SPIRIT ON ITS RETURN VISIT.

In March, 1828, without demonstrations, noises or preliminary warning, one evening while John Jr., sat reading as usual, a voice which he recognized at once as that most often used by the Spirit said, "John, I am in hopes you will not be as angry at me on this visit as you were on my last. I shall do nothing to cause you offense; I have been in the West Indies for seven years, and—"

John interrupted to say to the Spirit, in the same stern way as before, "Wherever you have been, or whatever you are, your proper place is in Hell, and the next visit you make you should go there and stay."

The Spirit took him seriously and told him it knew he would not understand why it came, that if he could he would know that some of the things it had done would at last result in the best for succeeding generations. "John, I am repeating this to you again and again, hoping you will see it." It said it knew that the death of his father in such a manner could but cast a gloom upon his son's life.

THE BELL WITCH

"You are telling me to go to Hell, John; such Spirits as I sometimes get a vacation, even banishment from their abode; but I will tell you there are thousands of human beings now living on this earth who are worse than I; they are only restrained by their fellow beings. If, after reaching their future abode, their Spirit could return to this earth, they would raise a thousand times more Hell than I have done. Don't forget that each one of you will have a Spirit, and that men on earth are best controlled through Spiritual influence. If this influence is not recognized finally, the world will be lost. As you think of me now, you would add millions of others to your thoughts and think a thousand times worse of most of them, if their Spirits came back on earth. There are Spirits millions of years old, John, that never have been connected with a body, but were created Spirits. Here on earth only the physical part of man, under mental control, is visible to his fellows. What a difference, John, if you knew what they are thinking! I know what you are thinking now."

John replied, "I want you to know what I am thinking. It is that I would give my life freely if I could tangibly grasp your form in my arms and crush you slowly, giving you the pain you caused my father scores of times, and then throw

THE BELL WITCH

you straight into the fires of Hell, if there be any such place. You would not be here if you did not know of your safety. I think you are thrice a demon Spirit; you belong to a world of demons; you come to this world where you cannot be harmed by its inhabitants. You are now neither of this world nor your own—a wandering thing between this world and some other; you must be as unhappy as you admit. I feel as if you would like to get back to your home, if they would let you stay there. You are too mean for them to wish to exist in your presence. I have repeatedly told you that I don't believe what you say of the good that will come of my father's punishment, and as often told you not to repeat it."

While John was talking, the Spirit said, "I am leaving you for the night. Just think over the things I have told you and be assured that I am willing to give you all the information I may possess. Let me know of the things you believe might result in some good."

As already mentioned, the Spirit did not like negroes; it could not understand how the Bells could tolerate them, and look after their comfort as they did.

To John, Jr., it asserted that it had known of Africa millions of years ago, and that parts of that country now covered by the jungles, and also parts of the Sahara desert, had been inhabited by a race of people superior to any the world had before or since known, and continued to be so civilized for thousands of years; then sunk so low in vice, corruption and cruelties to each other that it was entirely destroyed and there remained not a vestige of human life for thousands and thousands of years; then came the negro and several other races of the lowest order of humanity. Some ten thousand years ago, Egypt developed a civilization that was superior to that of this country. Carthage and a few others attained a high degree of civilization, no account of which is in your histories; this was long before your histories began. The Spirit then said that the most unfortunate occurrence in the history of the United States would be a war between the States, resulting in making the negro slaves as free as their present masters. It said that it had already been so determined by the Director of All Things; and with all its dislike for the negro race, it would agree with John that while the loss would be great to the South, that in the end it would be better to free the negroes.

John Jr., believed if it could be so agreed that the negroes' owners be paid for them they should be freed when it would not be a social evil, which would be many years. He himself did not think

THE BELL WITCH

slavery could go on indefinitely in the United States, yet he thought the negroes brought to the United States and made slaves had been much improved by their contact with civilized people. He assured the Spirit that he knew just as much of the negroes in his own country, as it did, and had no cause for such dislike of them as it had shown; that the most barbarous negroes in Africa would become less cruel and saner in their actions after six months slavery in Robertson county than it displayed toward his father and Betsy. There was no answer whatever to this charge.

The next evening the Spirit came while John was reading over the plans of the battle of New Orleans, which were at once recognized by the Spirit.

It said, "There will be another battle at New Orleans in the war spoken of last night. The city will be captured by a Tennessean; he is an officer in the U. S. Navy now, but he will be on the other side. This fight at New Orleans will determine you to go into the army against the North, but you will not realize your decision. You will depart from this world just after that battle at the city in which you have felt so interested.

John interrupted to say that he might depart shortly if there was any prospect of the Spirit remaining long.

THE BELL WITCH

Without notice of the interruption, the Spirit continued: "You fought at New Orleans the veterans who were soldiers against Napoleon in Europe. Their attempts against you Americans were extremely pitiful. Why was this? John, the Americans were trained in the great outdoors; they had absorbed the spirit of their country; they knew exactly what a rifle was made for; they knew to **aim at something.** The target in this case was a British soldier; their practice had made their aim deadly; their spirit gave them the same coolness as yours. You could shoot a turkey's head off at one hundred yards, and so could many others. It is at what you are aiming, then the accuracy of the aim that counts in your world. Those British soldiers were machines, simply taught to fire in the direction of the enemy, finely drilled, but not for the battle at New Orleans. If Wellington's and Blucher's armies, which defeated Napoleon at Waterloo, had both been at New Orleans, and their antagonist had been the same American force, with a simple addition of ten thousand men, they would have been disastrously defeated. It was foreordained that the English were to be whipped, and their foe was prepared for just such a battle. The hundreds of English soldiers who fell behind their dead comrades to save their own lives were not cowards; they simply recognized what their commanders seemed not to understand, that the Americans had aid which they could not overcome."

John Jr., replied, "Yes, we had aid; good eyes and long practice at rifle shooting; our bodies were fairly well covered; the British came forward in plain view and were easily hit. As to why they were so foolhardy as to make the assault, I do not know; they were attempting the impossible. That they would be defeated was easily foreseen by all our men."

"Yes, John, easily foreseen; but you fail to say why an English general failed to foresee that which backwoods American soldiers plainly saw. Pakenham threw away the lives of hundreds of soldiers and his own life in such a way that the human side of mankind can never understand the cause, the utter lack of military reasoning of the able English general. The cause was beyond the human understanding. He was led to destruction by an irresistible force."

John replied: "No doubt a soldier fights best when he has a good cause, and is in his own country. Our soldiers had constantly in mind what it would mean for the city to be taken; not just the destruction of property, but there were many French people in New Orleans, and we knew the English hatred for them, and had fears for them,

THE BELL WITCH

which added to our determination to drive them back. I am hoping your prophecy of that city's capture will never come true. I am sorry the subject came up."

The Spirit said in the history of all countries, there have been wars and always will be. There are times when it is best to fight it out and quit quarreling.

At the next conference the Spirit said, "The United States will have wars, no doubt in your time, but with the exception of the one spoken of, a result of which will be the negroes' freedom, these wars will not be serious until a great war which will likely involve nearly the whole world will occur. The United States at that time will have become one of the world's greatest nations; therefore, will be drawn into this terrible struggle. Millions of men will be killed, countries left in financial straits, and years of suffering invade every nation. Many people, as usual when wars occur, will for the time profit and become accustomed to a life of gain and luxury, and forget what the after results of such a great conflict must inevitably cause. Your country will suffer morally, financially, spiritually, and thousands actually will suffer from want of the necessities of life. Again, I am telling you that it can never recover except by a complete spiritual adjustment.

THE BELL WITCH

For some time after this great war there will be threats and signs of another great upheaval, which if it comes will be far more devastating and fearful in character than the one the world thought too terrible for the mind to grasp. Don't for a moment believe that men alone can adjust the world's affairs at that time. You are being told **now** that your country would have to be entirely different from all other great countries if there is not a revolution. It may not be one of blood, but such as the great Roman government had to undergo even before its fall. That government, the greatest ever known in this world, fell through the greed and the meanness of the rich oppressing the poor. All laws were for the benefit of the rich; finally Rome had only citizens who were either mere slaves or rich. The all-important part of Roman history is that the followers of Jesus Christ were persecuted under Roman governors; the Roman government ended. The Christian religion followed the Roman greatness; they are now firmly established all over the world, long after Rome's greatest rulers have been forgotten, the humblest of the leaders in Christianity are having sermons preached from their sayings; some of these followers of Jesus Christ were Romans. The greatest quality the Roman had was tenacity; once the Christians converted a Roman he stayed so and converted others. If Rome had been a follower of Jesus Christ nineteen hundred years ago, on to the date of the decline of their government, they would not have fallen. Selfishness, licentious habits, oppression of the poor, the rich profiting on the suffering of the poor ultimately leads to the downfall of any country. I have seen it for some millions of years. Your country will be tried out. You may be sure there will be a great social change, and the government itself will undergo trials unexpected; it should be equal to this great trial. I shall be there at that time; there will be thousands of Spirits unrecognized. As to whether your world continues and recovers, or ends, will depend upon whether the minds of men receive favorably the thoughts given to them spiritually, and unselfishly strive from the highest to the lowest, not merely to recover financially, but each strive to uplift his fellow man and bring the country back to Jesus Christ. Your preachers have at all times, as a class, been your best men, but they can do more harm than any others. Some will at that time outspokenly deny the divinity of Jesus Christ, even deny that there is a Heaven or Hell. There can be no doubt of the serious damage of such a belief; the world should never become converted to the doctrine that sin will not be punished, both here and here-

THE BELL WITCH

after. Preachers will tell you of "the unpardonable sin"—yes, there are many **unpardoned** sins, because of the sinners' attitude, but God Almighty can pardon any sin He wishes. Millions of years ago all human beings, after arriving at the stage where they had reason, knew that God Almighty could do **anything.**"

When asked if it could explain a reason for it being allowed on earth when God could quickly banish it, the reply was, "There is a reason for my appearance here again, and if you will think with the thinking power, of which you are capable, you will know at once. On my first visit here, people thought the things I did were most unheard of and not of value; the very fact that I could talk was a subject of wonder. What I am telling is no greater wonder than things people thought of me when I was here before; but the vast importance of what is being told to you will seem incredible when given to the world; its very seriousness will render it doubtful other than to men of the highest intellectuality, whose minds have wondered on these same things. Many centuries ago there were nations which believed the world's inhabitants were from Heaven, having been sent here because they were not yet prepared to associate with Angels, but were here for further preparation. Now, do not conclude those

THE BELL WITCH

people to be the most unaccountable imbeciles ever on earth, when you will have people in the United States who believe themselves quite intelligent preachers, yet will, as told you heretofore, disbelieve in Heaven and Hell, and the Divinity of Jesus Christ! When they reject the gospel of Jesus Christ, that will be as unpardonable as any sin committed. The best of theologians will come to this conclusion; they must if the world is to be saved after the plans of the Creator."

The Spirit was asked, "How can one believe you when you say you have seen things happening repeatedly for millions of years?"

"Yes," it rejoined, "I have seen over and over again, things happening in the same country for millions of years; the human mind cannot grasp the meaning of always, eternity, or the infinity of space. A Spirit such as you are listening to is a perpetual creation, not bounded by space or time, created by a power to whom this world must bow as The Infinite Being. This Being must be accepted by a faith that only can be realized by a being possessed of a soul and that soul regenerated by acceptance of Christ as the Saviour of men; His Spirit has endured and will endure for all time, even after this world has ceased to be. Now, the people of this world must not forget, this world will surely come to an end. If the sci-

THE BELL WITCH

entists will dig under the right parts of the earth's surface they will find the remains of destroyed civilization hundreds of thousands of years ago. Where your farm is now, the land was covered by the sea; where the sea is now, once was land and a civilized people; all gone, destroyed millions of years ago. That the world can be destroyed by its Creator at any time or by any means He chooses, should bring the world of sinners to their knees; its destruction can be complete within a few minutes. At no time will the inhabitants of the world, as a whole, believe there will be an end to the world; at the time when they think least of it, the end will come. Worlds many times larger than this have been destroyed so suddenly that it was only like a powder pan flash. No being can foretell when the end of a world will be, or if it will be so complete a destruction as never to be habitable again; it would only be a matter of opinion to say that this world will be completely destroyed; it can only be said, as already stated, that all the habitable part of this world has been destroyed. Do not for one instant doubt what is being told you; there is certain to come a time when what is being said to you will be proven. There are those who would sneer at it if you were to tell them should that time be at hand, and the best they could do would be to go down on their knees and be prompt in doing so. You are not being told this because there are statements in Scriptures of the world coming to an end; that was discussed with your preachers seven years ago. What is said to you now is what is expected, judging absolutely from past observation. Truly, your world is not yet worth destroying; the present population of the world does not compare intellectually or otherwise, with that of other remote days, long ago destroyed. When a world becomes so enlightened that there are no more inventions worth having, and the poor become helpless and starving, the rich thinking only of themselves, and suffering becomes so widespread over the world that the Creator will no longer permit it, then prepare for the end. When this world is destroyed again, it would seem that it will be complete destruction and never again be habitable."

The next evening the Spirit continued: "Have you digested that which was told you last night?"

John replied that it was wholly indigestible to him and he could not comprehend it all.

"That was just as expected. Why should a human be told worth-while things? It has rarely amounted to anything if told them; valuable things pass their understanding; and you just remember that there are so many things that cannot be understood now that you will be told only a few. You are not credulous, but just pass these things on and there will come a time when there will be more intelligence on this earth, as to how it is used will be the important factor. Great church buildings will be erected, and those occupying the church, in many instances, will think that enough, just to give the Lord a fine building; but their minds and hearts are not engaged in helping some one else. The great Catholic Church saved the Christian religion, through the dark ages; yet the edifices built by them have been so gorgeous and costly that it is not Christlike. **That money** could have been better placed in helping the poor, and building modest buildings; that idea, though, will continue, but there is no doubt that a Christian community, with a church building of moderate cost and occupied by real Christians, will be more pleasing to the Almighty than a magnificent building with numerous poor in the same neighborhood. There will be numerous Christians at the time we are contemplating, but far more real sinners who are giving no thought to others; they will have every opportunity of knowing of the Spiritual conditions, yet not accept the only hope for the world. Again, too many human beings will doubt that the Creator created man; they are attempting to say now that they were not created—well, that point was

THE BELL WITCH

theorized over. When the world was peopled by the beings told you of, they felt satisfied over their scientific conclusions, the present inhabitants will have their origin and creation all reasoned out; it does not help any to know more than that God created them and when He likes will destroy for all time those who are not prepared to go. Do not think this presumptuous for such a Spirit as I to be telling you of these things; the Creator has used the devil himself in his plans, and can use anything he wishes. He may be using me—I do not know—for the time I am to be here; let us hope I may be used in a way that may help future generations; they will need help, for as surely as the world now stands, those living at the time we have discussed will live longer in a few years than any of their ancestors, including those of Bible times, ever lived; they will have such responsibilities that they themselves will feel crushed and worn out. America is an old country inhabited millions of years before your people ever heard of it by a superior race; they were destroyed to be succeeded by others; they underwent the hardships and struggles accompanying the building of a great civilization. They had the wonderful buildings, great schools and mighty machinery that this era will acquire before it passes, but all that did not prevent their

THE BELL WITCH

destruction, along with all their worldly goods. Their scientists told them of how long the world had stood; that it would not last forever, but so many millions of years that they need not think of it. **You** are being told the facts—at the very height of their civilization, both North and South America were destroyed, likewise all inhabitable portions of the earth, and John, the largest portion was inhabited by a civilization far superior to any now on earth. They were destroyed by a quavering and shaking of the earth, so mighty that where oceans had been, there became dry land; where valleys and beautiful fields had been, there became oceans; a general leveling, upheaval and change of the entire surface of the earth. After all this came the other races, lower, yet they succeeded in becoming highly civilized. It has always been a question to the world's inhabitants as to where they came from. It is much more important as to where they are going. Their stay will be longer there. It would be useless to go into this with you further than to say men do not know how they got here and never will know; as to where they are going, millions will be uncertain. To you, in the presence of The Great Creator, is being said that to those who have been told the things of their chance for future happiness and reject its offer, there can be no reason for complaint if they suffer everlasting loss of their souls. There can be no reason for their Creator driving human beings into accepting eternal peace. They have been created with a mind and made free to accept or reject anything they like or dislike. Human beings have forced religious doctrines upon their fellow men, but they were in no way carrying out the Creator's plans when this was done. There are now countries that have State Churches, a certain Church being recognized by the State; there has been a time when this was a means by which some of the best people might be persecuted. Now look over the European countries and you will see that a few of these are far behind the world in education and Christianity; and as time goes on, if their Church and State rule is not abolished, they will be still further behind. Some of these very countries will, within the next century, prohibit religion of any kind being taught; will abolish the missionary organizations formed in their country; will allow all kinds of sins that are unlawful in this country; at that time the whole world will be near the ultimate finish. There will be organizations teaching no forms of government now known, and no religion of any kind; they will consider that to be religious is to be superstitious, that the real goal is to get all out of life while here. There will be nothing to

THE BELL WITCH

anticipate or fear after death; and do not forget, this country will have great numbers of the same kind; for all these people everywhere, Jesus Christ gave up his life that they might be saved; they will think little and what they do will be their own philosophy; their preachers will become too much inclined to philosophy and passing changes, forgetting that to be a pastor is the important role for a preacher. Great philosophers have been of value, but the quotation from Rousseau, "Socrates died like a philosopher, Jesus Christ like a God," should be thought of when mentioning Socrates or other philosophers in sermons."

"Once again, the being speaking to you is well acquainted with the facts. Jesus Christ died as your Bible teaches; that he was dead, buried, and arose, is just as true as that you were born. Thousands of Spirits, if allowed to talk, could tell you of that day. After millions of years, knowing of cruelties on earth, that to which Jesus Christ was subjected was the most affecting ever witnessed by the Spirit world, both good and demon Spirits. He had withstood the temptations offered by the devil, and died a God when he could have destroyed his torturers instantly. There are now millions of men who believe themselves capable of judging Christ, and there will be many millions more in years to come who will say the great acts performed by Jesus Christ, which are told of in the Bible, are not true, and that he was not the being he claimed to be. Pontius Pilate permitted the crucifixion of Jesus Christ, **knowing him to be innocent**; those denying Christ are as sinful. Pilate was a weakling, scared into the crime by the Jewish priests who were determined that Christ must die. The high priest Caiaphas was the compelling influence; he knew of Pilate's fears for the safety of his political position, and when threatened to disclose to Tiberius the fact that Pilate personally wished Christ to go unpunished and did not wish to give him up to the priest, like most politicians would have done, Pilate gave him up to be crucified. He knew the unrelenting character of those Jews who were opposed to Christ; he had generally given way to them, and now as the politician that he was, as a political expedient, he committed the never-to-be-forgotten heartless act of allowing Christ to be crucified for no other reason than to influence the priest to give a report to Tiberius favorable to himself Men should remember, when attempting to judge Jesus Christ, what became of Pontius Pilate. Within a comparatively short time after the crucifixion Pilate was ordered to Rome to answer charges preferred against him by the Jews on other crimes. Tiberius died before he arrived at Rome. On account of the worry over his many crimes Pilate committed suicide. Now, John, your preachers have not told what became of the actual murderer of Christ—Caiaphas, who led Pilate to believe that Tiberius, the Roman emperor, would censure him if Christ was liberated. No human can tell you what came of Caiaphas; there was no record of his death. I shall only say to you, Jesus Christ ascended and is more glorious today than ever; Caiaphas **descended.** You tell me that my fellow demons banished me; think of this Caiaphas and be assured that they have not **banished him;** he is still there and **always will be.** While Christ was living many men denied his divinity; the Jews were God's chosen people; yet Jews were his greatest enemies, but remember, John, there was a purpose for it all, and the Jews have been too unmercifully persecuted. There is coming a time when many Jews will be the world's most earnest Christians. Men may preach all the religious doctrines they can invent, but now and for all time the foundation of it all to be pleasing in the sight of the Creator must be love for your fellowmen. At the great and critical time to which has been indicated this world is to come, it cannot be repeated too often and emphasized too much that the lack of love for one another will be the worst situation and must be corrected, or the world will be destroyed; its Creator judging that to be the best for those who are following his commandments. There will be more than a billion of the world's population who are not following the Creator's spiritual laws. Why should he not, in justice to the few hundred millions who are, take them on to everlasting peace and obliterate those who put aside his offers of eternal life? The Almighty Creator's own people can scarcely live happily if their world continues in such a rebellious spirit and utter lack of the spiritual feelings and actions so necessary for their happiness."

"There will come a time when the food growing conditions of the world will change; if the world is not destroyed before that time. There will be drouths and floods as in the Bible times. The world will be unfortunate in that there will be no man whose prayers for rains will be answered. If men before that time will heed the warnings of nature and no longer destroy the natural growths; they may continue to reap harvests, but that they will not do. At that time men will heed nothing but science and finances, and the misery following will be fearful for you to contemplate. I have seen it happen before when the most fertile areas of the world became barren. The misery following was most appalling. The

THE BELL WITCH

Great Uncreated Creator has these methods of showing men that he rules the world."

John Bell, Jr., then said to his son: "At no time have the things told you ever been repeated to any human. I have followed a policy of never talking about the Spirit; I could tell you hundreds of acts performed by the Spirit while here that would likely interest people by their very seeming impossibility. You have been told only those things which appear to be of great importance in 1935. I do not believe the Spirit will appear as it did in our home; to perform the things it told me it would have to be everywhere at all times. I think the country will have reached a stage in its history that Spiritual conditions must improve (so often said by the Spirit) that good Spirits must manifest themselves daily in the actions of good people; that people must acknowledge their obligations and recognize they have a spirit. Taking the Spirit's words and studying very carefully its real meaning, I am of the opinion that it predicted a great cataclysm in or about 1935; that it thought the United States would be the most influential country in the world; that the government of the United States would be powerful in its efforts to avert the impending calamity. I am unable to say with exactness what the Spir-

THE BELL WITCH

it's real predictions were as to the final results, but it certainly gave grave predictions for that time.

It told me it would leave on the next night, after having spent several months with me. Frank Miles was invited (by me) to be present, promptly at 8 o'clock, the Spirit appeared. Addressing itself to both of us, saying, "To you two, who are inseparable friends, I say that whether the world ever hears of what I have told John or not, as bad as you both think I have been, I hope it will be recognized that what I have said to John is for the best, and the world will so live. I shall be there; you two will know what I am doing; the world may not recognize Spirits, whether good or demon; both will be here; it will have many of each. Again, John, your descendants will not be worried by me, but I promise you now if it is for their good, and I am allowed, for once I will be helpful to them and their country. I am bidding you and Frank a last farewell. I will be here again in another seven years, to which one hundred will be added."

"That was the last we ever saw or heard of the Spirit. It would be difficult for one not hearing the Spirit or being present at some of its performances, to believe what has often been repeated of it by as good and truthful men as ever lived.

THE BELL WITCH

I would not believe it at all if I had not seen it and had been told by others who heard it, if I had not known these witnesses so well. To no one else but you do I believe it important to tell of the Spirit's talks with me, the most remarkable of all. At no time have I attempted to influence any one's belief regarding this visitor; but to you I regard it a duty to say what I have and to point out that there is nothing to cause disbelief in the things told me. Certainly there is reason to believe that the world was created many hundreds of millions of years ago; and still more reason to believe that the Creator would not have waited until a few thousand years ago to populate it. I have not compared the Spirit's talks with the Bible, as much as it wished, yet to you I admit that if we believe the Bible we must accept the statements of there being Spirits both good and demon; and I do not mean just at the time the Bible was written, but also **now.** If the Bible, in its passages referring to man as being with a hope of eternal life, was true, then it means **now also.** We read of Angels; they are certainly **good Spirits;** if we do not believe there are Angels, we do not accept the Bible statements. It can not be that Angels are not created Spirits, that they have always been; they were not here always; nor do I know if all Angels were created Angels; if some

THE BELL WITCH

other Spirits become Angels. If we do not accept the Bible's teachings and believe there are Spirits, then we must lose hopes of a hereafter, the material body of man goes nowhere. Just when human beings go to Heaven, I admit without hesitation, that I do not know. With all the Spirit's cruelty when visiting our home, it displayed a wonderful knowledge of the future, and it always told of man's hope for the future; I am compelled to say that this being, with all, gave its statements with such accuracy on matters which I knew was humanly impossible, and afterword learned were true, that I am forced to believe the unheard-of things told me. That terrible times it predicted will come, I do not doubt; I hope the world will meet these times as suggested. As I have just said, I do not expect the Spirit to appear as before, but I believe it will be as it stated. At that time the world will have need of spiritual aid and there will be thousands of spirits here.

I am telling you these opinions the Spirit gave me of the final end of the world, not knowing of the real value of its prophecies, but telling you so that in the event it might be a forewarning by which people may be better prepared. The Uncreated Creator millions of years ago arranged that the world to be inhabited should be suitable for the beings placed upon it. Temperature has been the greatest factor in deciding a planet's habitation. For millions of years this world was too hot for human habitation. The first human beings were of a very low order, as told you before. The Spirit predicted the world would become too hot for human beings to exist, and the heat would increase so rapidly that it would be untenable for human beings in a short time, then suddenly it would be completely destroyed by a mighty explosion. It told me of this several times, as I have indicated; it never thought the majority of people would believe this prediction, but was solicitous that before that time came people should have an opportunity of knowing what it had said. The destruction at the time it was indicated would be complete; as to the world ever becoming inhabitable again, it would not say, nor did it give an exact date of the end.

I tell you the most indelible impression ever made upon my soul was the almost eye-seeing account the Spirit gave of the crucifixion of Jesus Christ, which I have no wish to describe; it was too heart-rending for me to call to your mind. I wish I could never think of it again. My life has been so saddened by this recital of the terrible torture of our Saviour that I can never get over it. When Jesus said on the cross, while suffering torture, "Father, forgive them, for they know

THE BELL WITCH

not what they do," he was so far removed from a human being that I cannot conceive of any man doubting his Divinity. God allowed him to suffer for a great purpose. Human beings suffer at times from their own sins, or just why they never know. I have no complaint to make of the experiences through which I have passed. To my descendants, I wish to say there will be no such harassing treatment as was given my father and sister Betsy; but the Spirit assured me some of them would know of its presence. You should pass these recollections on to your direct descendants, and at such a time as will help the world. Let them be known; until then admonish your descendants to withhold these recollections, and to add this advice, never forget that the United States government is now and will be in their time the best government in the world, and with the Spiritual aid of its citizens will surmount, if possible, any difficulties that may arise, so far as governments are concerned."

CHAPTER IX

RECOLLECTIONS OF DR. JOEL THOMAS BELL

J. T. Bell said that immediately after his father, John Bell Jr., gave these recollections to him he also advised him that he had been told many other things, but considered these the ones of greatest value. J. T. Bell then for the first and last time asked his father about subjects which he thought would be of great interest to know. In answer to the question, if the Spirit told him there was a real Hell fire, he said he had asked the Spirit that question and the answer was, "John, you have wished to strangle me and throw me into Hell fire; there is no real fire. I have every reason to know, but do not ever forget, as I told you often, there is an eternal punishment for those who are lost according to the sins committed while here on earth."

In answer to the question, if any soul ever escaped from Hell, the answer was, "Thousands of Spirits visit this world whose abode is Hell; men are prompted daily to do hellish acts by such Spirits; some have been banished, but are as unhappy as when they were in Hell."

THE BELL WITCH

In answer to the question, if men have been created so many hundreds of millions of years, and all had souls, and if they continue going to Heaven and Hell, will there be room for them, his father told him that he had discussed that with the Spirit and the Spirit had told him, "John, neither your mind nor the mind of any human being can understand what the Creator can do. Think of the distance of the most distant planet from this earth, then of others you can not see; think of the boundless space in this universe, and there **are other universes**; think of the room in space, but even then you are not able to grasp it. I shall not answer your question; if I did you would not understand, and it was not God's intention for you to know until that time comes. Study your Bible; it is not for me to tell you other than I have told you. I do not know all things, and if I did I would not be permitted to tell you."

In answer to the question, will there come a time on earth when men's lives will be lengthened to great ages as in Bible times, the answer was, "No; the world will come to an end at a time when men's lives have been shortened by the pressure of their way of living. This I have told you before. Think of it seriously. The fight for means of living will shorten men's lives, without a doubt."

THE BELL WITCH

J. T. Bell said to his father, "We speak of Angels usually as good spirits. We have been taught that Satan is the leader of fallen Angels. Is that the interpretation the Spirit gave?"

John Jr., said the Spirit had told him, "The descriptions you have had of the devil—Satan—and fallen Angels have been of such a character as to cause uncertainty in your mind as to the reality of such a being; Satan is the director of fallen spirits and will finally be punished still further for all the deviltry he has done."

The answer to the question, will the resurrection of the dead be at the end of time, or will they go to Heaven or Hell at once, was, "I believe the soul leaves the body at once, but there will be a final resurrection when the dead shall be raised; when all souls will be gathered together; just how this wonderful change shall be accomplished you are unable to comprehend, and I am not able to answer your question with exactness. It will be the last work for man's salvation that Christ will undertake. That time has not come. The Great Creator will determine how and when it is to be. I have never witnessed a Judgment day. I have told you of earthly things. There are things that will come to pass in the future world of man that I am not permitted to tell."

In answer to a question, did the Spirit tell you

THE BELL WITCH

that other worlds than this were inhabited by people such as live on this earth, John Jr., said it told him that other worlds were inhabited by people who had undergone similar trials as ours; some of these, as stated, had been completely destroyed, never to be inhabited again.

Dr. J. T. Bell said he thought if people would follow the recollections of John Bell Jr., as written, the world would be much better. He also thought that among the greatest poems, dealing with man's spiritual history, the Book of Job equals the best. Job knew he was not a sinful man and when his body was tortured, he asked God to tell him why he should undergo such suffering, knowing that the spirit of humanity was beyond his knowledge. Read the lamentations of Job, study the course of his life. Could you believe otherwise than he was greater for his afflictions, and that men have been made better by reading Job's life? Read of the suffering of John Bell; study his life and afflictions, not forgetting that he at no time lost faith in his Creator and was completely resigned to a fate he did not understand. Comparing this life to Job's, the conclusion must follow that there was a reason for his suffering that will be productive of good.

The author believes that the time has now come when the same spiritual assistance can bring

THE BELL WITCH

order from the chaotic conditions into which the world is now plunged. "These are the times that try men's souls."

The whole world must bow in acknowledgement to man's possession of a soul. A few doctors have said they dissected the human body and have never found a soul that they could see. These doctors could as well have said they did not find a mind. They certainly did not see it. There are nerve cells in the minute anatomy of man's brain composed of structures, the quality of which give him a mind of reasoning power, placing him above the lower animals. This reasoning power constitutes him a responsible being. If he does not use the mind given him in the way his Creator would have him, he will suffer.

The Spirit visiting the Bells was correct in its statements that the world is millions of years old and that arts and mechanical devices were lost thousands of years ago which could not be duplicated at the time of the statement. This has been proven by scientific investigation during the past few years.

The Spirit said these great advances were made, then completely lost, destroyed, and forgotten. We can not be so sure that we can go on under present conditions. Thousands of years from now scientists may be delving into our his-

THE BELL WITCH

tory to find that what followed us for thousands of years were mediocre human beings. All our great inventions may be gone, lost perhaps on account of a world cataclysm, or perhaps entirely destroyed as the Spirit described to John Jr.

If the Spirit which visited the Bells can be of any value to the world, let us hope that it may return in 1935, as promised. The author is of the opinion, as was John Bell Jr., that this return will be made in a different way. We will only recognize that there is a great spiritual effort being made to save mankind.

The Spirit assured John Bell Jr., that it would make itself known to a Bell descendant of his, as it did to him. The author would be the logical Bell upon whom this honor should be conferred, he being the only living son of John Bell Jr.'s, oldest son. It was estimated by John Jr., and J. T. Bell that the return visit would be some time in the fall of 1935.

One of the prophecies made by the Spirit in conference with John Bell Jr., was on a subject and of a nature of vital importance to the citizens of Tennessee and the entire nation, but it is not deemed best to tell it at this time. When the time seems best for the interest of the people, it will be offered for publication.

The

BELL WITCH
of
MIDDLE TENNESSEE

By
HARRIET PARKS MILLER

LEAF-CHRONICLE PUBLISHING CO.
CLARKSVILLE, TENN.

1930

TO THE READER

The writer is aware that the enlightened age of the Twentieth century forbids belief in witches.

In defense of what will be said in the following pages, I will say that my data has been secured from reliable people, some of whom visited the Bell home, and went away mystified as to what they saw and heard, and in consequence thereof they found it impossible to dismiss the whole thing as a delusion or hallucination.

CONTENTS

CHAPTER I

A mysterious agency that terrorized the Bell family of Robertson county, Tennessee, during the early part of the Nineteenth century, causing the death of Mr. John Bell, and partially wrecking the early life of his beautiful daughter, Betsy Bell.

CHAPTER II

Joel Bell, youngest son of John Bell, and one of the most reliable citizens of Middle Tennessee, tells of thrilling experience with the witch, and also tells why it was called "Kate."

CHAPTER III

The story of pretty Betsy Bell, who next to her good old father, was most tormented by the witch, which did everything possible to thwart her marriage to her handsome lover, Joshua Gardner.

CHAPTER IV

A. L. Johnson, familiarly known as "Sandy" Johnson, worked in Bell home, and tells of flatboating produce to New Orleans. During one of his trips, while camping one night on the river, he went ashore to catch a fat hen that had escaped from the coops on the boat; in climbing under a deserted house near the bank, something nabbed him fiercely in the back.

His first thought was that the Bell witch had followed him, but it later proved to be an old sitting goose, resenting his intrusion on her private domain.

CHAPTER V

"Deserted Surrency."

Thrilling story, almost equal to that of Bell Witch, told to the late Col. A. S. Colyar of Nashville, by a prominent railroad lawyer, who, anxious that facts concerning same be given greater publicity, was influential in sending Mrs. I. K. Reno (Itty Kitty Reno), a fine writer of Nashville, Tennessee, to a small village in southern Georgia, where she obtained facts, and on her return, wrote it up for the Nashville Banner—May 13, 1905.

CHAPTER VI

Witch tells of burying large sums of money, in silver and gold, at a spring on Bell premises. Men went in good faith to dig for it but found nothing.

Witch enjoys her ruse of fooling the diggers.

Dislikes negroes and plays painful tricks on them.

CHAPTER VII

Amusing stories told of eccentric Kate Batts.

Death of John Bell, supposed to have been caused from taking contents of a vial of dark medicine found on table near his bed.

Neither doctor, nurses, nor members of his family, could account for its presence on the table.

Following Mr. Bell's death, Betsy and Joshua renew hope of torment ceasing.

CHAPTER VIII

Easter Sunday, April, 1821.

A party met at the Bell home, and planned a picnic the following day at the "Enchanted Spring" on Red river.

Witch reappears, and casts a shadow over the occasion.

CHAPTER I

"THEY COME WHEN NIGHTS ARE HOARSE WITH WIND,
   AND DRENCHED WITH GUSTS OF RAIN,
AND SCRATCH WITH POINTED FINGER NAILS
   AGAINST THE WINDOW PANE."

During the early twenties of the past century, a mystery known as The Bell Witch appeared in Robertson county, Tenn., near what is at present the little town of Adams.

It was an invisible agency of tangible action, with a voice that spoke at a nerve-racking pitch when displeased, while at other times it sang and talked in low musical tones.

It seemed bent on tormenting two members of the Bell family, Mr. John Bell and his beautiful daughter, Betsy, hence the name Bell Witch.

The writer is aware that the enlightenment of the twentieth century forbids belief in witch stories, but when we recall the testimonies of the best citizens of Robertson and Montgomery counties, who visited the Bell home during the witch activities, we are forced to conclude it was something beyond human understanding.

Among some of those citizens whose worthy descendants are with us today were the Carneys, Forts, Norfleets, Northingtons, etc. Elder Reuben Ross and Elder Sugg Fort, pioneer Baptist preachers, visited the scene and came away mystified, but owing to their responsible positions, as ministers of the gospel, they thought best to be quiet on the subject, and spoke evasively to those who interrogated them as to what they heard while on the Bell premises.

Years after his famous duel with Dickerson, near Adairville, Ky., General Andrew Jackson came over a portion of the same road on his way to Robertson county to satisfy his mind as to what he had heard of the Bell Witch. He brought with him several horsemen and a four-horse covered wagon, laden with provisions, bedding and tents, prepared to spend a week. When within a few hundred yards of the Bell home, and driving along a nice smooth road, some member of the Jackson party spoke slightly of the Witch, when the wagon wheels suddenly refused to move.

The driver whooped and whipped, but the big strong team seemed powerless to move the wheels. After they had worried some time, a sharp metallic voice rang out from the bushes, saying, "All right, General, let the wagon move on, I will see you again tonight." And it kept its promise. The Witch was out in full force, singing, swearing, pulling cover from the beds, slapping and pinching pretty Betsy Bell till she screamed with the pain. The Jackson party did not sleep a wink, and when morning came they were ready to go home, with no thought of even unfolding their tent.

Nashville friends, knowing the intentions of the General's trip, and also his previous skepticism as to the existence of the so-called Witch, were surprised to see him back so soon and began plying him with questions as to what he saw and heard, at the Bell home, to which he replied: "By the Eternal, I saw nothing, but I heard enough to convince me that I'd rather fight the British than to deal with this torment they call the Bell Witch."

A great common danger draws people together and people came from everywhere, some drawn by curiosity, but the majority through sympathy for the Bell family. The long lane leading up to the Bell home was filled with horses hitched in every corner.

For a long time the Bell family kept the mystery a secret and when they finally confided it to intimate friends, they referred to it as "Our Family Trouble." The news of the great mystery spread and emigrant wagons came from several Southern states, laden with people anxious to know of something more than hearsay, regarding the Bell Witch.

News went out at first that the strange sounds were a species of ventriloquism practiced for mercenary purposes by certain members of the Bell family, but this theory did not hold good in view of the fact that Mr. Bell and his daughter, through its agency, suffered untold torture.

Owing to the effeminate voice of the Bell Witch, the mystery was generally referred to as proceedings from an invisible something of feminine gender. In a future chapter I will tell of her name, "Kate," and why it was given. Nothing counts in valuable history against vivid recollection truthfully told.

Among the prominent Montgomery countians who visited the Bell home during the Witch's activities was the late Felix Northington, of Port Royal. Mr. Northington was born in 1802 and was 16 years old when the Witch made its first appearance in Robertson county. In speaking of it, Mr. Northington said:

"I was especially interested in what I had heard regarding the Witch from the fact that my father, Samuel Northington, and John Bell both emigrated to Middle Tennessee from North Carolina and settled within a few miles of each other in Robertson and Montgomery counties. Then, too, my wife's relative by marriage, Dr. Hopson, of Port Royal, was John Bell's family physician and was called at all hours, day or night, to attend Mr. Bell while he was being tortured by the Witch, and on several occasions I accompanied him.

"On my first trip, I recall meeting the late George Wimberly, grandfather of A. B. Killebrew, of Clarksville. Mr. Wimberly met us at the front gate, and I asked, 'Well, George, what have you seen or heard?' To which he replied, 'Oh, nothing more than hearing a sound as if some one were throwing rocks against the house from the outside, and when we went out to investigate, the noise continued, with no cause to be seen. I'm going a short distance across Red river to see my sick brother, Joe Wimberly, and will make another trip when the Witch has a more exciting performance on hand.'"

Mr. Northington continued, "We went in and Dr. Hobson examined Mr. Bell and finding him suffering not only great bodily pain but extreme nervousness. He applied mustard plasters and gave a soothing potion to quiet his nerves. Soon thereafter a shrill voice rang out from a three-cornered press in a corner near Mr. Bell's bed: "Ha, ha, ha, Doctor, you had just as well be throwing your medicine in the fire, as to the good it will do old John Bell, for I'll see to it that he gets no peace of mind or body as long as he stays in this world, and more than that, I'm going to torment the life out of his daughter, Betsy, if she doesn't quit going with that good for nothing Joshua Gardner.' Joshua Gardner was a fine young man and pretty Betsy Bell's first suitor, but for some unknown reason the Witch seemed bent on wrecking their future happiness.

"We spent two hours in the Bell home and returned to Port Royal, finding a group of citizens awaiting us, in front of the old hotel that stood at the end of the street leading down to the Sulphur Fork creek ford. Several of the group plied Dr. Hobson with questions regarding Mr. Bell's case, and he expressed grave fears as to the result of his strange symptoms, one of which was a feeling in his mouth as if he were gagged with a stick sharpened at each end extending midway across his tongue, with the sharp ends piercing his jaws from the inside. So distinct was the feeling that he had Mrs. Bell to look in his mouth to see if there really was anything, but she found nothing.

It may be well, in the beginning, to state that the Witch claimed to have come from North Carolina, and said she would make headquarters at the Bell home, remaining until her desired mission was fulfilled.

Major Garaldus Pickering, grandfather of Mr. D. G. Elliott and Mr. Harry Pickering, of Clarksville, was a noted educator of the early twenties. He taught in Robertson county. Several of Mr. John Bell's sons were his pupils and he was often in the Bell home and told some wonderful experiences witnessed there in connection with the Witch. It was said of Professor Pickering that he tried hard to disabuse his mind of anything akin to superstition and when his pupils were excited and aroused over the Bell Witch stories, he admonished them to be quiet and encouraged them to hope and believe the mystery would be satisfactorily solved. The Bell brothers, pupils of Professor Pickering, hung on his words with eagerness, not knowing when they too, might become victims of the Witch's wrath.

CHAPTER II

October, 1884, Cumberland Association held its annual three days' session with Harmony Baptist church of Robertson county. Dr. A. D. Sears, pastor of the Baptist church of Clarksville, Tenn., and Mr. Joel Bell, a prominent lay member of Springfield church, both being advanced in years, were appointed a home with Dr. J. T. Darden, a good Methodist friend, who lived nearer the church than some of the Baptist members. This was ten years before the history of the noted Bell Witch was written in book form by M. V. Ingram of Clarksville.

There were other guests in the Darden home, besides the worthy delegates above mentioned, among them a young man who had always been interested in anything pertaining to the Robertson county mystery. The name Bell led the young man to ask the venerable delegate, Mr. Joel Bell, if he knew anything of the Bell Witch, to which he gravely replied:

"Yes, my young friend, I have heard of it to my sorrow, for I am the youngest son of the late John Bell, who was tortured to death by what he termed 'our family trouble.' "

Now, it was generally known throughout the country that certain surviving members of the Bell family were sensitive on the subject, and Mrs. Darden and Dr. Sears, both possessing refinement of the highest order, felt embarrassed that the Witch subject had been mentioned, but since it had, there was nothing to do but to sit and listen.

They felt somewhat relieved, however, when "Uncle Joel," as he was familiarly called, assured them that he had never taken offense at reasonable questions concerning the Witch, and since the subject had been broached he would tell a few things that came under his youthful observation.

He said: "One night we four brothers were sleeping upstairs, John and Drewry were in one bed, Richard Williams and I in another. About 10 o'clock, after I had been asleep perhaps half an hour, I was suddenly awakened by a strange feeling in my hair, as of some one trying to twist it out by the roots, catching it by handfuls and twisting, followed by quick, powerful jerks that increased in force till I felt like the next would take the top of my head off. I screamed; mother and father sleeping in a downstairs room ran up to know the trouble. My brothers, sleeping in the same room, experienced the same feeling, though their suffering was not so intense as mine.

Just across the hall from our upstairs room, sister Betsy slept and from the way she screamed her suffering must have been unbearable; mother and father carried her downstairs to sleep the remainder of the night. I followed.

"I will never forget how sister Betsy looked as she sat there trembling in every limb and her heavy suite of blonde hair tangled and twisted as though it could never be straightened again."

Mr. Joel Bell, at this date (1884) was the only survivor of the immediate Bell family who had walked and talked, face to face, with the so-called Bell Witch. He was the youngest child of Mr. and Mrs. John Bell and was 14 or 15 years old when the above experience occurred.

Dr. Sears, in his characteristic dignified manner, was an interested listener, and if he felt skeptical as to what he had just heard no one ever knew it, for he had been long and intimately associated with Mr. Joel Bell in religious affairs, and could not doubt his word in this instance.

A few years later, they had occasion to meet in a series of revival meetings at Red river church at Adams, and by mutual agreement, one autumn afternoon drove together out to the old Bell homestead site, a short distance from town. There was nothing there to indicate that it had once been the home of a prosperous pioneer farmer, save the fine clover fields surrounding the tumbled down stone chimney piles, a fast decaying pear orchard, and the family graveyard, 300 or 400 yards north of the old home site.

During this trip Mr. Bell made no reference to the Witch. It had been some time since he had visited the family graveyard, and the sight of his parents' graves awakened memories sweet and tender, and while Dr. Sears copied in a note book the inscriptions on their monuments, Mr. Bell related incidents of their Christian lives, and how he received his first religious impressions from the prayer meetings, song services and other religious gatherings held in his father's home.

Mrs. Kate Batts, of Robertson county, was a very eccentric woman. Her husband was a hopeless cripple the greater part of his life and she assumed control of his business. She was exacting in all her dealings with men and thought everybody was trying to cheat her.

In a business deal with Mr. John Bell soon after he came here from North Carolina, she accused him of treating her unfairly and swore vengeance against him. In passing his home on her way to old Red River church, of which she was a member, she was heard to remark one day, "Oh, yes, old John Bell, you have your broad acres, and your comfortable home, and the future may look bright to you now, but just wait and see what sad changes are soon coming to you and a certain member of your family."

Rev. James Gunn, a highly esteemed minister of the neighborhood, was often in the Bell home to offer comfort and sympathy to the much disturbed family, and on one occasion when the Witch began talking, he ventured to ask what it was, to which it replied: "Brother Gunn, I believe you are a good man, and I will not tell you a lie, I am Kate Batts' Witch. You just watch her pretty close, and you will see and hear her do many things that will convince you that she is a witch. She begs every woman she meets to give her a brass pin and when she gets as many as she wants, she puts them on a stump in John Bell's woods, and tells me to use them.

"Haven't you seen that old long-legged devil, writhe and twist and say that something was sticking pins all over him?"

True it was, that such had been the case.

We cite another incident that led many to believe that Mrs. Batts was possessed of an evil spirit. It was churning day at a near neighbor's; the good housewife churned faithfully, but no signs of butter; growing impatient, she exclaimed: "I verily believe old Kate Batts has bewitched this milk and I'm going to burn her out," so she plunged a red hot iron poker into the milk and set the churn aside.

Having occasion to step across a field to the nearby Batts home she found Mrs. Batts sitting in the corner nursing a badly burned hand, the result a few moments before of handling through mistake the wrong end of a red hot poker.

The Witch's interview with Rev. Gunn regarding its identity was widely circulated and poor Mrs. Batts, let her be ever so innocent, was shunned by a certain element of the neighborhood. From this time on it was called "Kate."

It seems that the mystery Witch or whatever it was, when being questioned as to who, or what it was, never told the same tale. On one occasion it said to a group of neighbors assembled at the Bell home: "I am a spirit who was once very happy, but I was disturbed, and now I am unhappy. I am the spirit of a person who was buried in the woods over yonder in sight; my grave was opened and my bones scattered; one of my teeth was lost under this house, and I am here looking for it."

Mr. Bell, a year or two before this, had some farm hands to clear a plot. They found mounds supposed to be Indian graves, and he directed them to leave them undisturbed.

Later, some neighbor boys thinking they could find valuable Indian relics, opened one of the graves, and finding nothing but bones, they kept a few of these, and among them a jawbone, which they carried to the Bell home, and while sitting in a hallway, threw it against the wall, the jar knocked out a tooth, which dropped through a crack in the floor.

Mr. Bell remembered the incident, and when the Witch mentioned the lost tooth, he had the floor torn up and sifted the dirt underneath, hoping to find it, but failed.

After the floor had been replaced a voice with a tone of derision proceeded from under the house, saying, "Ha, ha, old Jack Bell, I just said that to see if you'd be big enough fool to look for that tooth."

For some unknown reason the Witch seemed very fond of Mrs. Bell, calling her by her Christian name, Lucy, and sometimes jestingly, "Old Luce." During the fall of 1820, Mrs. Bell was stricken with a severe spell of pleurisy; she was sick several weeks and during the time Kate was on hand every day to offer a word of sympathy, such as "Luce, poor Luce, I'm so sorry you are sick. What can I do for you, Luce?" When Mrs. Bell was nervous and restless from extreme suffering, the Witch would command quiet that she might take a nap and rest, and on several occasions she would say, "Luce, let me sing you a sweet song. I can sing in a way that will soothe your nerves better than a houseful of old quack Dr. Hopson's medicines. Don't you know Hobson is a humbug?" "No, Kate, I thought he was all right. Sing me one of your sweet songs, and we'll talk about Dr. Hopson another time."

The Witch sang two beautiful songs and members of the family in an adjoining room gave way to tears, feeling that Mrs. Bell's funeral hymns were being sung, for she was critically ill. The following day Rev. Sugg Fort went to visit Mrs. Bell; she was a member of his church, Red River, and he esteemed her as one of his best members; he was accompanied by his son, the late Lawson Fort, who told the writer the following:

"We had been in Mrs. Bell's room a short while, long enough for father to offer a short prayer, when we heard a voice like that of a woman in an upper room just over Mrs. Bell's bed, 'Luce, I've been to the woods, to get you some grapes, you must eat something, hold your hands.' Mrs. Bell replied that she was too weak to hold her hands, but that she loved grapes. In a moment two fine bunches of wild summer grapes rested on the table near her bed. There was no crack or opening in the floor overhead through which the grapes could have fallen, and we saw no hand place them on the table.

"Father was astounded," said Mr. Fort, "and on our way home he said: 'Now, Lawson, my son, I would advise you not to mention anything we saw or heard in the Bell home regarding the Witch. You went to pay the Bell brothers a friendly visit and I went on a religious mission to a sick sister, and it will not be becoming in either of us to give publicity to anything that will add to the Bell Witch sensation.'"

Long years after Rev. Sugg Fort had passed into the Beyond his discreet advice lingered with this same son, who on several occasions, even as late as the early '80's refused offers of liberal pay, from newspapers and magazines for reliable data known to be in his possession.

The reader will observe in perusing the Bell Witch story, that the Bell family, comprising six generations who have lived in Robertson and Montgomery counties, have been people of the highest order and that they, nor their intimate friends, to whom they confided "Their Family Trouble," have shown inclination to give it any savor of sensationalism."

(The Mrs. Batts referred to above s not related to the Batts family now living in Robertson county).

CHAPTER III

"Mid woodland bowers and grassy dell
 Dwelt pretty, blue eyed Betsy Bell.
 But elfin phantoms cursed the dell,
 And sylvan witches all unseen
 Wielded sceptre o'er this queen."

Before proceeding further with the Bell Witch story, generally conceded to be the wonder of the Nineteenth Century, and unexplained mystery of the world, the writer will speak more in detail of what might be termed the heroine of the story.

Elizabeth Bell, commonly called "Betsy," was born in 1805. Of the nine children of Mr. and Mrs. John Bell, there were seven sons and two daughters, Esther and Betsy.

Betsy was the youngest of the two sisters, and the pet of the household, especially after the marriage of her sister to Bennett Porter.

On the outskirts of Mr. John Bell's thousand-acre farm, he built a commodious school house of nicely hewn logs, and employed what he knew to be the best teachers, usually gentlemen teachers, who boarded in the Bell home. Among the latter was Prof. Richard Powell, between 25 and 30 years of age, and referred to in the neighborhood as "The

Bachelor Teacher." Several of the Bell children were his pupils. Betsy entered his school at 10 years of age, and remained four years, or as long as he taught at the same place.

As she ripened into beautiful young girlhood, the teacher bowed to her charms, but kept quiet, save an occasional expression to Mrs. Bell, who in the meantime had observed his growing admiration for her young daughter.

Among Prof. Powell's pupils was a handsome young man about 18 years of age, Joshua Gardner. Young Mr. Gardner was not only handsome, but he was intelligent, and descended from a fine family. He and the Bell boys were companionable, and he was a frequent visitor in their home. It was about this time that the Witch activities began in earnest, and Mr. Gardner tried in every conceivable way to help solve the mystery. His first personal encounter, however, was one night about midnight, while sleeping in an upstairs room, he felt something begin to pull the cover from his bed. It began pulling first from the foot of the bed, increasing in force till all the top cover was pulled off, no power in sight being able to retain the cover when once the effort was made to remove it. Determined, if possible, to successfully cope with the mystery, the next night Mr. Gardner invited Mr. Frank Miles, a substantial citizen, and a man of powerful physique, to spend the night with him in the same room, and requested Mrs. Bell to furnish for their bed the newest and strongest covering she possessed. About the same hour, as the preceding night, the cover-pulling performance began, and the bed was stripped. Next began the pulling gently of the pillows from under their heads, followed by pulling at the bolster, when the latter was felt, Mr. Miles grew defiant and exclaimed, "See here Miss Witch, or whatever you be, I'll give you a tussle over this bolster, for I'm tired of this one-sided affair." Suiting the action to his words, he flung his 225 avoirdupois midway across the bolster to no avail, down it went to the floor!

As to physical strength Mr. Miles was a champion, the writer, when a child, saw him crack a large black walnut between his teeth as easily as an ordinary person would crack a hazelnut. At the Witch's victory in the cover pulling episode, it was said that Mr. Miles was chagrined, for it was the first time in his life he had been outdone in the exercise of his strength. Accompanied by other neighbors and friends, he continued to spend many nights in the Bell home. His sympathy for the family was great, and he went so far as to suggest that Mr. Bell sell his large estate in Robertson county and move to some distant parts.

Soon after this interested suggestion from Mr. Miles, Kate the Witch, appeared in great glee one night, when a group of friends had assembled in the Bell home. She opened the conversation by saying: "Hello, Frank Miles, you are on hand again, are you? Let me say to you, that you needn't waste your breath advising old Jack Bell to run away from me, for I can follow him to the end of the world."

An amusing incident in connection with the Witch pulling cover from the Beds in the Bell home, was told to the writer by T. S. Hamlett, a highly esteemed citizen of Port Royal. Mr. Hamlett heard the story direct from the lips of his grandfather, Capt. James Hamlett, a veteran of the War of 1812, born 1796, and died 1888 in his ninety-second year.

During the Bell Witch excitement in Robertson county, Captain Hamlett was married to Miss Mary Jane Atkins, of District 5, east Montgomery county. They began housekeeping at a little cottage home, on the Hopson estate near Port Royal. Among the bridal presents received by the young couple was a white home-made counterpane. The wedding took place during the summer months, and being a strong advocate of fresh air and proper ventilation, the front door of the Hamlett cottage stood open at night. Away into the night, one night, Capt. Hamlett was awakened by a slight pulling of the cover from toward the foot of the bed. The pulling grew stronger and stronger; his first thought was of the Bell Witch.

It happened that they were sleeping under the new home-spun counterpane which was very strong in texture. He determined to hold it on at all hazards and gripped his end of the cover with both hands. Every now and then, an unusual jerk from the foot almost wrenched it from his grasp, but he held on, till he felt his grip weakening, when he suddenly decided on quick action. He bounded to the floor, still holding on to the cover, falling over chairs and other household furniture in a wild rush for the open door, through which a stray yearling calf had entered and indulged its bovine propensity, by chewing a liberal portion of the valuable counterpane into shreds.

The author of the above story is buried at Greenwood cemetery, Clarksville, Tenn., and is doubtless the only veteran of the War of 1812, whose dust reposes there.

It was said of Captain Hamlett that he greatly enjoyed telling a joke at his own expense.

As time passed handsome young Joshua Gardner grew more attentive to pretty Betsy Bell.

It was a balmy June afternoon, when he called at her father's home; a dozen or more young people had assembled on the front lawn. Soon he and Betsy as usual withdrew from the main crowd.

Scarcely had they settled down to a comfortable seat under a large pear tree when they heard a voice from a large field fronting the Bell residence. At first it was hardly audible, but gradually approached nearer and still nearer, till they distinctly heard in pleading tones, "Please, Betsy Bell, don't marry Joshua Gardner! Please, Betsy Bell, don't marry Joshua Gardner!" Soon the voice died away in the distance, going in the same direction from whence it came.

Betsy shuddered, believing it a premonition of something that would blight her life. Gallant young Gardner, brave and stout of heart, tried to relieve her fear. They were engaged and but for the interference of this unsolved mystery, a bright future was before them. Seeing the cloud that hung over her beautiful young life, her relatives and friends did all they could to make her happy. They gave social functions in their homes, had fishing parties on the banks of Red river and when these diversions failed to give relief, accompanied by a favorite girl friend, she was sent to visit relatives in Southern Kentucky, but the Witch followed her and her fine, sensitive nature led her to believe or fear, that she was an unwelcome visitor in any home. With this belief she seldom left her father's roof for a visit of more than a day's length.

Until this stage of our story, Kate the Witch, had seemed to exist only in sound and invisible force, but daily growing more aggressive, she assumed form. One day Betsy went with some children to a near-by forest to gather spring blossoms to decorate for Easter Sunday. In a short time she returned with no flowers and looked nervous and agitated. Her mother inquired the cause. Not wishing the children to hear her gruesome story, she beckoned Mrs. Bell to follow her to a private room, where she spoke as follows:

"As I reached overhead to break off dogwood boughs for the children, a voice spoke, 'Betsy Bell, don't break a flower; if you do, you will pay well for it.'

"I looked and twenty feet from me across a wagon road running through the woods, I saw, as distinctly as I see you, a ghostly looking woman, dressed in pale green, suspended from the limb of a large red oak tree. She was holding on with both hands, and her frail figure swayed in midair.

"At first I hoped it was an illusion or distracted vision of mine, and I turned away, but when I looked the second time, it was the same. I hastened home with the children, all the while watching them closely to see if they noticed anything unusual, but they did not. They wondered why I did not get the flowers we went for, but I evaded giving the real reason.

"Mother, I am a strong believer in retribution and just here I want to ask if you have ever heard of any evil deeds committed in our family?

"You know the Bible speaks of the sins of parents being visited on the children for several succeeding generations. I have wondered if a remote ancestor in North Carolina had possibly done something that was causing this family trouble in Tennessee."

"No, my dear daughter, if there has ever been a stain or blot on either my family or your father's, I never heard of it.

"The Bells take great pride in their record for honesty and fair dealing. Only yesterday I heard your father denouncing some rascality going on in the vicinity of Port Royal."

The above reference to Port Royal deserves the following explanation. Like all newly settled counties, some who came here from the old North State found bands of law-breakers, principally horse thieves, and owing to the latter, it was difficult for the large land owners to keep good horses. The legal authorities seemed powerless to detect and punish the offenders, so the situation demanded active and strenuous methods on the part of the best citizens of Robertson and Montgomery counties.

Sulphur Fork creek at Port Royal is the dividing line between the two counties, hence their interests were one and the same. The Forts, Gunns, Johnsons, Bells, etc., took the matter in hand and organized vigilance committees, which as a whole formed an organization termed Regulators. The members were not numerous, but they were fine judges of human nature, and were no respecters of persons when it came to a matter of finding and punishing a criminal.

In the near-home case in question, the ring leaders of the horse-stealing gang, much to the regret and surprise of the Regulators belonged to good families, one of whom lived in Red River Bend below Port Royal, and the other just across the state line, over in the edge of Kentucky.

The Regulators met in solemn council over at Patrick McGowan's home and decided as the two leaders of the horse-stealing gang lived six or eight miles apart, they would bring them together on what they termed "half-way ground to receive proper punishment. The place was selected near where Sadlersville now stands. The criminals were brought in, accompanied each by three Regulators. They were partially stripped of their clothing and swung side by side to the lower limbs of a large red oak tree. Switches from the tough hickories and beeches were in readiness, and laid on with strong arms and determined wills that meant business. When the chairman of the humane committee cried, "Hold, it is enough!" the two men were taken down and warned to leave the country within the next three days. They obeyed promptly, and it was several years before they were again heard from, apparently leading respectable lives in two Southern states.

Apropos of the horse stealing period above mentioned, the following may be of local interest. During the early '70's, the writer spent several days with relatives at Rossview, and during the pleasant visit I received a message from an uncle, the late E. L. Fort, of Robertson county, saying that he wished to visit once more the scenes of his young manhood spent among the Wimberly's of that section, and would come for me at a certain date and led along with him a favorite saddle horse, "Kate," for me to ride home, horseback riding at that date being popular.

A mile or two beyond Port Royal on our return home, we branched off from the main highway, coming a nearer route by what at that time was Col. James Lockert's home—a picturesque spot overlooking the second Horseshoe Bend in Red river. On nearing the front gate, Mr. Fort reined up his horse and said: "In that house lives one of the bravest men that ever shouldered arms to fight for the Confederacy—Col. Lockert, of the 14th Tennessee Regiment.

"My brother-in-law, James S. Dancey, went out with Col. Lockert and was killed in battle at Culpepper Court House, Va., 1862. Mr. John Hurst, of Clarksville, Tenn., was standing near when Mr. Dancey received his mortal wound, and kindly sent details of his death to distressed relatives of Tennessee."

Coming on several hundred yards this side of Col. Lockert's residence, Mr. Fort paused again, and directed my attention to a ravine on the right of where we stood. The place was seemingly several hundred feet below the regular highway over which we were riding.

"That place," he said, "in the early twenties was the hiding place for stolen horses, and the famous Bell Witch gave information that led to the arrest of two of the principal leaders of the horse thieves." He mentioned a fine horse that was stolen from his father, Rev. Sugg Fort, which was afterwards found near Graysville, Ky., and restored to the owner.

CHAPTER IV.

Among the credible citizens who gave me information concerning the Bell Witch, I would mention the late A. L. Johnson, familiarly known as Sandy Johnson, of District No. 1, Montgomery county, father of the late Captain R. Y. Johnson. Mr. Johnson was born in Louisa county, Va., in 1803, and came to Graysville, Ky., near what is now Guthrie, at 15 years of age, a penniless orphan boy.

Being of an industrious turn, he at once set about to find work. He heard that Mr. Bell was having extensive clearing done on his large landed estate in Robertson county. On reaching there, he found two of the Bell Brotehrs—John, Jr., and Drew—engaged in building flat boats on Red river, near where the Sugg Fort mill was later built, and only a few miles from the noted Bell home. At that date people were engaged in flat-boating having no other means of transporting their produce, except by wagon trains.

The boats were built during the summer and fall seasons, and cabled to trees along the river bank, waiting for the winter and spring rise in the river, when the boats were loaded with produce of every kind, and when the tide and current were sufficient to float the crafts, they were loosed from their moorings, and started on their long trips. A few hours' float carried them to the Cumberland, from there to the Ohio, then to the Mississippi and on to New Orleans, the great Southern market place. Treir cargo consisted of bacon, butter, eggs, dried fruit, whisky and large coops of chickens, ducks, guineas and turkeys. They usually tried to reach New Orleans a few days before Christmas, in order to get the holiday prices for their produce. Each boat was manned by three persons, two at the oars on each side and one at the end to steer the direction and warn them of dangerous obstructions, as snags, breakers, etc. They camped at night on the river banks, striking camp about sunset in order to cook supper before dark.

One evening soon after they had cabled their crafts to trees, a large fat chicken hen spied a broken slat in her coop, flew to the shore and took refuge under a seemingly deserted cabin nearby. The boys cast lots as to who should catch her, and the job fell to young Johnson. Divesting himself of his coat, he carefully crawled under the cabin and caught the hen, who squawked a lusty squawk, and while giving her neck a twist or two, as a quietus, something grabbed him in the back about where his home-made suspenders crossed; his first thought was of the Bell Witch, and next a rattlesnake; when in truth, it proved to be nothing worse than an old setting goose resenting his intrusion on her private domain.

After selling their cargo at a nice profit, and receiving drafts on a Nashville bank they turned homeward, walking a good portion of the way.

After several months' association in the flat boating business, young Johnson and the Bell brothers became warm friends and he continued to work for them, and during the time, saw and heard much pertaining to the Witch, that he told the writer sixty years later.

Among the remarkable things he told was of the visit to the Bell home of a stranger from the East, who professed to be a Witch killer and hearing of the notorious Bell Witch, came to try his hand on its extermination. He gave his name as Jack Busby and brought with him his witch-killing gun, in which he used charmed silver bullets. He spent a week and during the time not a sound was heard from Kate. Mr. Bell was encouraged to hope the man really had some power over witches and thought of making him a proposition to remain permanently on his premises. It was the longest rest the Bells had enjoyed.

Mr. Busby told them he was sure Kate was afraid of him and that as important business called him home, he would go and attend to same and return to Robertson county if they later found it necessary. His horse was brought to the front gate, Mr. Bell accompanying him to bid him goodbye. He mounted, but the horse would not budge. Busby spurred and whipped to no avail. It suddenly reared on its hind legs and fell backward (the rider barely escaping serious injury.) It rolled, kicked and squealed as if in great pain, when the exaspering voice of Kate rang out, "I can make that horse go, old quack Busby. Let me get on behind," after which the horse dashed off, kicking and squealing like a wild animal. After going a mile or two, however, he quieted down and went on his way like any other horse.

Mr. Bell, in the meantime, nervously walking up and down the front yard, discouraged and dumbfounded heard Kate hilariously exclaim: "Ah, ha, old

Jack, your witch killer didn't seem to get a shot at me with his silver bullets. On the other hand, I got the best of the job, for I filled his old bald-faced horse's hide full of brass pins. Ha, ha, ha! how the old devil did rear and kick, but I took them out before he reached the end of the lane. I did enough to convince him that he needn't come back again."

As yet the reader has not been informed that besides the personal recollections of reliable people contemporary with the Bell Witch and handed down to the younger generations, that a faithful record was also kept by Richard Williams Bell, one of the seven Bell brothers. It was in the form of a diary labeled "Our Family Trouble," and sacredly guarded as a document, that at some future date might be instrumental in solving the mystery. Williams Bell was the best educated member of the family, or of the nine children of Mr. and Mrs. John Bell, hence he was chosen to keep the record.

Various attempts (some reported not to have been honorable), were made to secure the Williams Bell manuscript, by people eager to turn it to mercenary account, but none succeeded till eighty years later, when the late M. V. Ingram, of Clarksville, a warm personal friend of the Bell family, obtained it from James Allen Bell, eldest son of Richard Williams Bell, and grandson of Mr. John Bell.

Mr. Ingram, through the kindly loan of the record, obtained data from which he wrote the Bell Witch story in book form, the latter receiving a wide circulation in many states.

Strange to say, very few of the books can now be found. Many years ago the writer was spending the summer at Bon Aqua Springs, a popular health resort in Hickman county. Among the hotel guests was a Mrs. Ezell, from West Tennessee, near Gardner' Station in Weakley county. On learning that I hailed from east Montgomery, she inquired if I had ever heard of the famous Bell Witch of Robertson county. I told her I had, and that I had also brought along with me a history of it in book form, written by M. V. Ingram, of Clarksville, Tenn. She was enthusiastic, and gave as a reason that she was a grand niece of Joshua Gardner, who left Robertson county on account of the Witch's persecution of pretty Betsy Bell to whom he was engaged and the wedding day appointed. I willingly loaned her the book. Next morning she came to breakfast unusually late, and excused her lateness by saying she had read the Bell Witch book the greater part of the night and considered it the most wonderful story she had ever read. I gave her the address of an agent who was selling the books at Port Royal and she ordered several copies sent to parties at Gardner's Station and Dresden, Tenn. ,

Among the Bon Aqua guests was the late Col. A. S. Colyar, an ex-Confederate jurist of Nashville. He was a fine raconteur, and the entertainment committee of the hotel requested that he give some Bell Witch stories at the auditorium, which he did with thrilling effect.

Among his interested listeners one evening was Judge John C. Ferris, who conducted an Orphans' Home and during the time found good homes for twenty-eight hundred orphan children. The venerable judge rose in the audience and said: "Colonel Colyar, I am going home tomorrow, and before I leave I have an earnest request to make of you, when you return to Nashville, please don't bring your Bell Witch stories to my large family of children. If you do, it will take all the soothing syrup in the state to quiet their tender nerves."

In one of Richard Williams Bell's records of "Our Family Trouble," as he termed the Witch mystery, he wrote as follows:

"After being tormented almost beyond human endurance, father had grown so miserable that he never walked alone about the premises. Early one morning, during the autumn of 1820, he requested me to go with him to his hog pen several hundred yards from the house. He wished to direct the hands in separating the porkers from the stock hogs.

"We had gone but a short distance from the house, when one of his shoes was jerked from his foot. I replaced it, tying the string in a double bow-knot. A few steps further on, the other shoe was jerked off in the same manner. I tied string of same in hard knot also. We finally reached the hog pen and he gave the desired directions as to the separation of the hogs and started back home, when both shoes were jerked off and thrown some distance ahead of us. He then complained of a sharp blow on his cheek, as if some one had slapped him with an open hand, the blow almost stunned him. He sat down on a log by the roadside; he was seized with terrible contortions of the body and his always pleasant face wore the expression of a demon! For the moment, I felt almost compelled to forsake my own father. Amidst all this, we could hear derisive songs and revilings.

"As the sounds died away in the distance, I saw tears on father's cheeks and faltering courage marked the wearied expression of his face, and he said, 'Oh, my son, I cannot much longer stand the persecutions of this terrible thing. It is killing me; I feel that the end is near, and I will welcome the day.' Sitting there on the log he lifted his voice to God in fervent prayer. He prayed for strength and courage to stand it, and asked if it were possible to let this affliction pass.

"After he had ceased praying a feeling of calm resignation seemed to come over him, but he was physically exhausted, and immediately on reaching the house he took his bed, and while he was able to be up and down for several weeks, he never left the house again."

Although shut in, he continued to take interest in his business affairs, and while he in no way doubted the ability of his dutiful sons, in the administration of his farming operations, he occasionally sent for Dean, a faithful Negro slave, to come to his room and talk over matters pertaining to his department of work. Dean and his mother Chloe, were given as a bridal present to Mrs. John Bell by her father, John Williams, of Edgecomb county, North Carolina, in 1782. He drove one of the big wagon teams that brought the Bells from North Carolina to middle Tennessee. He was trustworthy and money could not buy him.

"The year 1820 was an unusually good crop year, and Mr. Bell's Red river bottom fields yielded a bountiful corn crop, from which he hoped to realise a nice profit by feeding it to his large herds of hogs and cattle.

One day he sent for Dean to come to his room and talk over the advisability of having a corn shucking. In ante-bellum times the big farmers had corn-shuckings, later called husking bees, on their premises. They were enjoyable occasions and profitable also as they enabled the landlords to get their corn in convenient feeding shape. Dean favored the idea, but advised Mr. Bell to invite a big crowd of white folks, giving as a reason that the Negroes of the neighborhood had heard of the Bell Witch, and were keeping pretty close to home at night. He told Mr. Bell of a remarkable experience he had a few nights before, while on his way to his wife's house at Alex Gunn's. The moon shone bright, and as he walked through the little skirt of woods, just after leaving home, something that looked like a big black dog, sat in the middle of the road just in front of him. It had two heads when he first looked at it, and in a few minutes it had no head at all, and ran off down the road making as much noise as a team of mules.

Seeing that Mr. Bell was growing nervous, Mrs. Bell suggested that they talk further of the proposed corn shucking. Dean was an expert rail splitter, and said he would have the rails ready on the grounds, for the building of the corn pens; he also had a nice lot of boards to cover them. As Dean left his master's room, a look of pleased satisfaction played over his dusky countenance, for he felt humble pride in being consulted regarding small business matters.

It was about the last of November. The corn was piled high near the big log corn crib, and new rail pens. About 100, mostly farmers, had been invited to attend a corn shucking at John Bell's, those living nearest bringing their whole families. They came at early candlelight; the women folk and children went to the house to be with Mrs. Bell, while the others went to work with a hearty good will. It was a cool, frosty night and a cheerful log fire lighted up one corner of the horse lot.

At corn shuckings they usually had what they called a heap walker, who walked over and around the corn heaps and sang the regulation corn song. For the singing of this, a smart, quick witted person was chosen, one who could cleverly fit into his songs, amusing local sayings. By a unanimous vote, Dean was elected. He would sing the verses alone, the crowd lustily joining in the chorus. The corn song ran something like this:

"Ginn erway de corn, boys, ginn erway de corn,
Done come here ter night fer ter ginn erway de corn,
Corn, cor-n, cor-n, cor-n, corn fer de Bell cow, corn fer de mule,
Ash cake fer de yaller gal, dat makes you all er fool,
Corn, corn, corn, dear ol Marster's corn."

The chorus went:
"Cor-n, cor-n, ginn erway de corn,
Gwine ter shuck it all dis night
As sho's yer bor-n, bor-n."

Along toward midnight they changed up from the corn song to the dram song. The finding of a red ear of corn always meant an extra dram, so the boys went to work with renewed vigor. The dram song ran:

"Dram, dram, little drop er dram, sir,
Dram, dram, fetch erlong de dram.
Come, come, little Mr. Whisky,
Nigger mighty thirsty, wants er little dram."

John Bell, Jr., was in modern parlance, master of ceremonies, and when the corn pile was finished, he came forward with his little speech of thanks to the hands for their good work, and a jug of whisky for which Robertson county had long been famous.

While the sweet old drams were liberally dispensed, there was no drunkenness. It was an old saying that day must never break on a corn shucking feast, so the boys marched three times around the house, sang a good-bye song to "Old Marster," and went to their respective homes. The corn shucking night was a pleasant diversion for the Bell family.

Handsome Joshua Gardner was on hand, and played the role of errand boy, rotating between the house and the corn heap, pretty Betsy Bell occasionally accompanying him, and hearing as usual the sweet old story he oft had told her.

Kate the Witch was not heard during the occasion, but made up for lost time later on.

CHAPTER V.

The late Col. A. S. Colyar, eminent jurist and statesman, of Nashville, Tenn., previously mentioned as being interested in the Bell Witch, said he grew less skeptical as to its existence after hearing of a similar mystery of a later date, which appeared in Southern Georgia, near Macon, in 1870.

Col. Colyar heard the story of "Deserted Surrency" from a prominent railroad lawyer, who had often visited the place, and was anxious that the facts concerning it be given greater publicity.

So Mrs. I. K. Reno, a talented writer of Nashville, Tenn., went to Georgia, and on her return wrote for the Nashville Banner of May 13, 1905, an authentic and thrilling story. I take the privilege of quoting from this story as follows:

"It was a journey of nearly 700 miles to the little village in Southern Georgia called 'Deserted Surrency,' which on account of the fierce onslaught of an invisible agency, had rendered the place unendurable to its few inhabitants, principal among whom was an influential family by the name of Surrency.

"Old Surrency, the original, was an estate or large plantation owned by the Surrencys, which later grew to be a small village of scattered houses, separated by varying distances. At the time of my visit the place had been deserted about thirty-five years.

"I was accompanied to the old homestead by Mr. Samuel D. Surrency, a gentleman of pleasant address and seemingly 50 or 55 years of age. He was the presiding magistrate in his neighborhood, and a citizen of high standing. The house was a double frame structure, two stories high, with a wing in the rear.

"The gates and outside doors were nailed together with boards, the shutters hung loosely from their hinges, the windows were broken, and the wind swept through the old house with a mournful sound as if lamenting its ruin and desolation.

"The special interest of the strange and mysterious drama which was enacted there thirty-five years ago, centered in the old house before which we stood. And there at my side stood Esq. Samuel Surrency ready to relate what had been a terrible reality to him and the entire family. He said:

" 'My father, A. P. Surrency, built the old house you see standing there, away back in the forties. His large family spent many happy years there, before the trouble came that drove us away.

" 'One summer afternoon, 1879, my mother was sewing in that first room to the left of the entrance to the old, old house there. She was unusually happy at that date. The older children were at home to spend their summer vacation, her household was well ordered, and father was in prosperous circumstances.

" 'Mother was of a calm, placid disposition, and not easily aroused by trifles. On this same afternoon that I mention, her attention was attracted by a strange noise from a wash stand in the room. She looked in the direction and saw a pitcher in the bowl on the washstand rocking back and forth.

" 'She went to see if a string or wire were attached to it, thinking it perhaps a boyish prank; finding none, she resumed her sewing, when she was amazed to see the pitcher lift itself several inches from the bowl, then settle down into it again, with a loud noise.

" 'Then the pitcher was lifted entirely out of the bowl and placed with deliberate care, beside it on the washstand.

" 'Immediately after this the bowl was flung from the washstand, and fell in fragments at mother's feet, and in quick succession the smaller pieces of the entire toilet set followed, adding their several little heaps to the debris on the floor. From that day the peace and quiet of the happy old homestead were destroyed.

" 'The next day, the family was eating dinner, when a door opening on the front gallery, and which was standing open, began to move slowly, and was shut with calm deliberation.

" 'That was done," said mother, quietly, "by the wind."

" 'But she had scarcely spoken when the door opened, and was flung back against the wall with great violence. At the same time two windows in the room were raised and lowered many times, breaking the panes into tiny bits.

" 'These were only small beginnings. Frequently during the meal hour, milk, tea, coffee and soup were flung into the faces of those at the table, several times inflicting painful scalds and burns. Spoons were broken, or suddenly twisted out of shape in their hands.

" 'At first the demonstrations were confined to the dining room and mother's bedroom, but after a few days they spread until there was not a room in the house free from the frightful phenomenon.

" 'At all hours of the day and night, the heavy old fashioned furniture would creak and groan, then as if moved by unseen giants, it would rush from its place in a mad dance about the room, and would either move quietly back to its accustomed place or would be dashed to splinters on the floor, with noise like a thunderbolt.

" 'One of the most singular phases of the phenomenon was the affect that the presence of the young daughter of the house, Miss Clementine Surrency, had upon the strange demonstrations. From the very beginning of the trouble it was noticed that when she was present, the manifestations were more potent and varied.

" 'Anything she chanced to lay her hands upon seemed drawn to her by some strange law of magnetism, and would follow her movements through the house, floating slowly through the air behind her, several feet from the floor, as if supported by invisible hands.

"'Her mere entrance into a room would frequently be cause sufficient to send all the furniture in its spinning around in a mad whirl, lasting several minutes, and would either end suddenly in profound quiet, or in a loud crash, wrecking some favorite heirloom.

"'Father and mother were thoroughly mystified and unhappy. They were constantly alarmed for their own and their children's safety, and having become unnerved, they were earnestly discussing the advisability of moving away, when something occurred that brought them to a sudden and definite decision.'

"Here Mr. Surrency, who had been talking all this time in a low monotone, raised his voice a trifle and pointing to the front room on the right entrance of the homestead, said with a vibrating tone of excitement in his voice: 'It occurred in there. That was our sitting room, and one afternoon in February, as I entered the hall, I glanced into the sitting room and saw my elder brother, Robert, sitting at a table reading.

"'A low fire was flickering in the open fireplace, and several logs which had burned through, had fallen apart and rolled from the andirons to the hearth.

"'I wished particularly to speak to my brother, and called to him, but he was so absorbed in his book he did not hear me. Just as I entered the room I noticed a commotion on the hearth, when to my surprise, I saw one of the huge andirons lift itself from the fire and began to move across the room. It gathered momentum as it went, and rose swiftly in the air till it reached the level of my brother's head when it dealt him a heavy blow on the temple.

" 'He sprang to his feet, stunned and bleeding, while I grasped the andiron in my hands, trying thus to shield my brother; but I may as well have essayed to hold a thunderbolt, for it wrenched itself free from my grasp and struck my brother again on the head.

" 'Run," I called to my brother, "run for your life! If you stay here you will be killed, and I cannot help you." The poor boy did run out of the room and the andiron followed, striking him heavy blows till the poor victim, covered with blood, fell unconscious at our mother's feet.

" 'Then the andiron moved slowly across the hall, and resumed its accustomed place on the hearth. The next day my father moved the entire family to his other farm. We took nothing with us but a few clothes, as the other house was furnished and father thought best to leave everything here undisturbed. A long illness followed my brother's frightful experience.

" 'The shock produced a fever which came near proving fatal.

" 'The move to the other farm gave us about ten day's rest when the trouble began again, and father had a small cottage built a short distance down the railroad, which really was the beginning of the little town, Surrency. While the new home was being built father and mother thought best to send their daughter, Clementine, away on a visit; the repeated shock had well nigh wrecked her nervous system.

" 'So father and I drove her over here one day for her to pack a trunk of clothes she had left here, and which she would need during her anticipated visit. She ran up to her old room, and father and I waited there on the front porch.

" 'She closed the outside shutters of the room and came below, saying the trunk was ready for us to bring down. At that moment we heard a noise, as if some heavy object was being dragged over the floor, then the crash of wood and glass, and the next moment my sister's trunk was lying on the lawn there, burst open and all her outfit torn to shreds.

" 'We made a thorough search through the house, but found it all locked and barred as we had left it a few months before, and it had remained untenanted. Yet my sister's trunk had been dragged across the floor and hurled through the closed sash and shutters by the same unseen agency which had, for nearly a year, destroyed the happiness of our home.

" 'The news of our singular misfortune spread far and wide, and people from all parts of the country came to see and investigate for themselves. Among the prominent Georgians who came for that purpose were Henry Grady, Bridges Smith and Henry Pendleton, editor of the Macon Telegraph. Soon after the Surrency family left the original homestead, Foster, the great clairvoyant and medium of that date, asked permission to spend a week in the deserted house; he was accompanied by friends who were also mediums and spiritualists.

" 'At the expiration of a week Mr. Foster made the following statement: "Mr. Surrency, I have witnessed all the phenomena which you have mentioned, under strictly test conditions, and I assure you they are due entirely to spirit control.

" "I saw no materializations, but I asked the spirits why they had driven you from your home, and through certain raps on the table, I received this reply:

" 'The entire Surrency family is strongly mediumistic, especially Miss Clementine Surrency; therefore we have sought to make them recognize our power, for we have need of them to deliver our message to the world.' "

The son, who gave the above facts to Mrs. Reno, said his parents did not live to be old, and he was sure their lives were shortened by the horrors enacted in their home by the unseen mystery. In conclusion, Mrs. Reno said:

"After taking leave of Mr. Surrency and I was once more on the 'limited' en route for Tennessee, I asked my friend, the railroad attorney, his opinion as to the strange story to which we had just listened.

" 'It is beyond explanation,' he replied. 'The fact that the Surrency family patiently endured their harrowing experiences for a year, and then, in desperation deliberately abandoned two homes, and also that the few surviving owners will not occupy them, or even cultivate the land surrounding them, prove very clearly that there must be many things on earth, of which our philosophy takes no heed.' "

CHAPTER VI.

A year had passed since the first appearance of the Witch. Several neighbors had come to spend the night with the Bells. It was warm weather, and most of them had repaired to the front porch, when the voice of Kate was heard asking: "Where is old Sugar Mouth?" Meaning Mr. James Johnson, a very consistent Christian gentleman of the neighborhood. "I want him to attend to some business for me, something that requires an honest man."

"I am at your service, Kate, what is it?" inquired Mr. Johnson.

"You know, as I've said before, I am anything and everything, here, there and everywhere. Just now I'm the spirit of an early emigrant; I brought a large sum of money in silver and gold from North Carolina and buried it for safe-keeping, at a big spring at the southwest corner of the Bell farm, the spring is near Red river and the money is under a big flat rock, near the spring. I was taken sick and died without ever telling any one where it was buried.

"I have come back to tell about it and to say that I want Betsy Bell to have every dollar of it. Drew Bell and Bennett Porter seem to work well together.

I want them to do the digging and old Sugar Mouth to count the money and take charge of it.

"I won't tell how much it is, but it's worth going after.

"Keep it a profound secret, and start to work early tomorrow morning. A strange man has come to the neighborhood looking for buried treasure; he has some mysterious way of finding it, and I want you to beat him to the spot."

The mysterious way referred to must have meant what today is termed necromancy, an art, or natural gift, by which a person of unusual magnetism may use what is called a divining rod, which enables him to locate underground streams of water, metals, etc.

Early next morning found the three men on their way to the spring, supplied with the necessary tools for digging.

They found the surroundings exactly as Kate had told them, and were soon making the dirt fly. Upon close examination they found the big flat rock was deeply embedded in the ground, and first thought of blasting it, when they recalled that Kate had enjoined secrecy in their operations.

After removing large amounts of dirt from under the stone, they cut large poles and used them as levers. After six hours of the hardest work they ever did, the stone was moved from its deep setting.

Finding nothing directly under it, they were not altogether discouraged, but continued to dig, thinking perhaps the money was buried far beneath and the stone was used as a marker and protection.

If possible, they continued to work with greater faith and earnestness. By way of resting each other they alternated, in work, first one then the other digging and removing loose dirt. After opening a hole six feet square and nearly as deep, with no money yet in sight and their tools seemingly getting heavier at every stroke, hungry and exhausted, they abandoned the job in disgust, and went home. That night Kate appeared in high glee, laughing and ridiculing the men for being so easily duped.

She repeated word for word how they talked and acted. "Bennett Porter sure is a digger," she said, "he staved that mattock up to the eye every pop, and oh, how it did make him sweat.

"Drew Bell handled dirt like a Trojan. His big old hands just suit for scooping dirt.

"Old Sugar Mouth didn't lend his tender hands, and I don't blame him, but he spoke some mighty encouraging words to the boys while they worked. Ha, ha, ha! I guess he thought he'd get a few dimes out of it."

Dean, the faithful Negro previously mentioned, worked in a river bottom field, several hundred yards from the spring. He had heard nothing of the digging for money.

Hot and tired from a hard day's work, on his return home, he went by the spring for a cool drink of water. He spied the great bank of fresh earth; his first thought pictured a dead man beneath. He took to his heels and fairly flew! It was generally known that the Witch hated Negroes and patrollers (white citizens of ante-bellum times, who patroled their respective neighborhoods at night to see that Negroes were obedient and law-abiding), were not needed in the section of Robertson county, adjacent to the Bell estate.

Dean had circulated some wonderful experiences with the Witch, some of which were reliable. Among "the home folks niggers," as he called them, was a younger brother, called Harry, a house boy in the Bell home.

Harry's first duty was the building of the big log fire in the family room. The Bells were early risers and Harry was expected to report for work a short while before daylight, but he grew negligent, and came later and later each day, till Mr. Bell threatened to whip him. Finally, Kate took the matter in hand and said, "Never mind, old Jack, I'll attend to that nigger."

A few mornings afterward, Harry was later than ever; realizing he was late, he hurriedly threw a big hickory back log across the massive andirons, put on his kindling and smaller wood, raked his bed of live coals (there were no matches at that time) to the front, and threw on a bunch of pine shavings, and got down on his all fours to blow the well arranged pile into a quick blaze. A fine pose for paddling in the right place presented itself to Kate, and she whipped him unmercifully. Harry yelled and begged for mercy.

Mr. and Mrs. Bell, still in bed in one corner of the room, heard the licks, which seemed to be laid on thick and fast with a paddle or broad strip of wood. After that, Harry was on time every morning.

While doing a lot of clearing in the virgin forests surrounding the Bell plantation, Mr. Bell had an old-time log rolling. After the day's work was done and the workers had assembled in the back yard waiting for supper, the youngsters of the crowd engaged in wrestling bouts and other athletic stunts. Among the latter was the difficult feat of locking their heels over the back of their necks.

Phyllis, a 12-year-old Negro girl, who waited in the house and assisted Aunt Lucy, her mother, in the kitchen, was a close observer of the back yard exercises, and the next day, she stole away upstairs to test her athletic capacity.

After several unsuccessful attempts, she suddenly realized that her feet had gone over her head, and were securely locked. Repeated calls from Aunt Lucy availed nothing. Phyllis answered from upstairs but never came. Finally the irate mother, armed with a good tough switch, started on the warpath, saying as she climbed the stairway, "Bound I kin fetch dat gal down dem stars." She pounced on her with vengeance, and dealt several keen blows, before poor Phyllis had time to explain that the Witch had locked her heels holding them tight and fast, till her mother appeared at the head of the stairs, when they were suddenly unlocked.

It is strange how so many people of the present generation, in talking of the noted Bell Witch, persist in the belief that it was nothing more than the art of ventriloquism practiced by Betsy Bell, the fair young daughter of doting parents.

A strangely inconsistent belief, from the fact that it manifested such dislike for her father, for which no cause was ever given, declaring its intention of killing him before leaving the place, which, from reliable testimony, it did.

John Bell, Jr., was also suspected in complicity with his sister, in the ventriloquism scheme, an unjust accusation which was denounced by the best people of that time. That the mysterious agency came near wrecking the early life of Betsy Bell, at an age when life meant most to her by opposing with dire threats her marriage to Joshua Gardner, one of the finest young men of the country, was proof positive that she was not guilty. Not only this, but her own physical suffering was evidence of her innocence. While her suffering was not to be compared to that of her father, it was bad enoguh.

She had no sign of hysteria, but on the contrary was of a stout, robust constitution. She was subject to what her mother termed "spells," which came on at regular hours, once or twice a week, late afternoons, often after dark, or about the time the Witch began her performances.

The spells often began by fainting followed by shortness of breath, panting, as if for life. They lasted on an average of twenty or thirty minutes, and the greater the effort to restore her, the more intense her suffering. The attacks usually left her lifeless and exhausted, for a short while, but when she did finally rally, she seemed perfectly normal. Strange to say, while the spells lasted, Kate was never heard to speak a word.

From the seeming interest that Kate took in religious affairs, when she first made her appearance, a few of the best people hoped that she had been

Divinely sent to work wonders, as a reformer. At that date, people were more susceptible to religious influences than they are today. The heads of homes erected family altars, and it was the custom for the neighbors to meet in each other's homes to engage in prayer, exhortation and Bible study.

Rev. James Johnson was the leader in such meetings. He was a consistent Methodist and Mr. John Bell was a Baptist, and active member of Red River church, the oldest Baptist church in Tennessee, organized 1791, by Elder Reuben Ross. There was no spirit of denominational jealousy in the community, and the good Christians mingled and worshipped together as Christians should, in every age and clime.

Kate the Witch on several occasions conducted religious services in the homes, equal to some of the best preachers. She could sing any song in the hymn books, the Psalmist was mostly used, and could quote Scripture from Geneiis to Revelation. She took delight in religious discussions, and always got the best of the argument, being ready with passages to sustain her point. Her knowledge of Scripture was mystifying.

One night a small congregation of people had assembled at the Bell home to hear a religious discussion in which Kate took part. The discussion turned on the command against coveteousness and theft, when a man present ventured the remark that he did not believe there was any sin in a hungry person stealing something to eat. Instantly Kate inquired: "Mr. Blank, did you eat that sheepskin?" (For discreet reasons we substitute the name Blank). Kate's question revivad an old scandal, almost forgotten, in which a certain party had stolen a nicely dressed sheepskin from a good old man who had intended to use it as a comfortable cushion for his saddle.

The Witch' wonderful knowledge of all things led many to inquire after important things necessary to be known. Sometimes the answer would come: "I don't know, wait a minute, I will go and see." A quick and correct report would be forthcoming. The above characteristic, if such it might be called, was discovered by the following incident:

Jesse, the eldest of the seven Bell brothers, lived within a mile of the old homestead. He had been absent some time, on a long journey, and was expected to return on a certain day. After supper of the same day, his anxious mother inquired if any of the family had been over to Jesse's or had heard anything of his return. Kate spoke promptly, saying: "Just wait a minute, Luce, I will go and see for you." Almost instantly the same voice replied: "Yes, Luce, Jesse is at home; he is sitting at a table reading by the light of a tallow candle." Next morning he came over to his father's and when told of the circumstance, said it was true. Said about the time his mother said she inquired of his return, there was a distinct rap on his door, and before he had time to see what was wanted the door opened and shut quickly, as if some one had suddenly peeped in and left. Mrs. Jesse Bell was frightened and said: "I do hope the Witch is not going to follow us to our quiet little home."

One night four strangers, desiring to hear something of the Bell Witch and its performances, arrived at John Bell's and before they had time to speak by way of introducing themselves, Kate announced one by name, exclaiming a loud voice: "This is the grand rascal who stole his wife; he pulled her out of her father's house through a back window one night, and hurt her arm and shoulder, making her cry, then he whispered: 'Hush, honey, don't cry, it will soon get well'."

The men remained several days, and before leaving, the party in question was asked if the Witch was correct as to his matrimonial escapade and he admitted that it was true to the letter.

CHAPTER VII.

In a former chapter we stated that the Bell Witch was called Kate for a very eccentric woman, Mrs. Kate Batts, who lived near the Bell home. On account of an unpleasant business transaction for which Mr. Bell was in no way to blame, she made dire threats as to his future.

Just who first gave the name to the mysterious agency, tradition does not say, but it was generally known throughout the country that Mrs. Batts was a creature far out of the ordinary and from her sayings and doings, she became second in notoriety to the Witch itself. Some time ago J. A. Edwards, the efficient letter carrier on Rural Route No. 1, leading out from Adams, and who lives near the famous Bell Witch scene, told an amusing story in which a near kinsman of his figured in connection with Mrs. Batts. Referring to the late M. V. Ingram's Bell Witch history, written in 1894, I find he corroborates the story as follows:

Mrs. Batts owned a valuable little bunch of Negroes. She kept the women employed mostly at spinning cotton, wool and flax, weaving jeans, linsey and linen, and knitting socks and stockings till late bedtime. She always had something in this line to sell. She would buy all the surplus wool rolls and other raw material needed in her business and this furnished her excuse for visiting regularly over the neighborhood. She was very aristocratic in her own conceit, believing as she did that her comfortable estate entitled her to move in the highest social circles.

She used high sounding, bombastic language, imitating as she thought the best educated people. On account of this she was subjected to much ridicule in the community. She kept an old gray horse expressly for the saddle. This animal was saddled every morning as regularly as the sun shone, though she was never known to ride. She invariably walked, carrying a copperas colored riding skirt on her left arm, two little Negro boys walking on each side, and Phyllis, her waiting maid, walking in front, leading the old gray mare.

This caravan was widely known as "Kate Batts' troop." No matter where she went, if entering the most elegantly furnished parlor in the country, she always spread the copperas colored riding skirt over the seat offered her, and sat on it.

With all her peculiarities and eccentricities, she was an earnest church worker, always expatiating on the Scripture, and the goodness of God, and would have her share of rejoicing in every meeting, and it never required an excess of spiritual animation to warm her up to business. She was a charter member of Red River Baptist church, and a regular attendant, always late, but in time to get happy before the meeting closed.

On one occasion, Rev. Thomas Felts, a devout Baptist minister, was conducting a revival meeting which had been in progress several days. A deep religious feeling had been stirred, and the house was crowded every day with anxious people.

One day, just as Parson Felts had finished preaching a rousing sermon, awakening sinners to repentance, and called mourners to the anxious seat, and the large congregation was engaged in singing rapturous praise, and transporting songs, the Batts troop arrived. Phyilis observing that "ole mistis" was filling up on glory as she caught the first notes of the singing, hurriedly hitched old Gray and rushed in. The house was pasked and the meeting had reached its highest tension.

The congregation stood singing. The interest centered around Joe Edwards, who was down on his allfours at the mourner's bench, praying for Divine forgiveness. Mr. Edwards in many respects was a good citizen, but in some ways he was a desperately wicked and undone sinner. Everyone was anxious to see him converted. The good brethren and sisters had gathered around, instructing and urging him on, and he seemed almost at the point of trusting. At this critical moment, Sister Kate Batts rushed up, elbowing her way to the altar. She deliberately spread her copperas riding skirt all over Joe Edwards and sat down on him. She was a large portly woman, weighing about 200. The poor man, not knowing what had happened, concluded he was in the last throes of the struggle with sin, and that the devil was on top.

In his desperation he cried aloud: "Oh, I am sinking! Take my burden, Jesus, and make Satan turn me loose, or I will go down and be eternally lost. Oh, save me, save me, blessed Lord." A good brother invited Sister Batts to a nearby seat, but she politely declined with her customary flourish of big words.

"No, thank you, this is so consoling to my disposition that I feel amply corrugated. I'm a very plain woman, and do love to homigate near the altar when the Lord is making confugation among the sinners."

"But, Sister Batts," continued the deacon, "the mourner is suffocating."

"Yes, bless Jesus, let him suffocate; he's getting closer to the Lord."

The situation had become both serious and ludicrous when Sister Batts suddenly felt the foundation beneath her giving away, and she was caught by two of the brethren, just in time to avert a still more ludicrous scene.

Joe Edwards rose up shouting joyfully for his deliverance. Sister Batts clasped her hands and shouted, "Bless the Lord, bless my soul, Jesus is so good to devolve His poor creatures from the consternation of Satan's mighty dexterity."

Rev. Felts took in the situation and, without seeming abrupt, dismissed his congregation, that the people suffering from suppressed laughter, might give open air vent to their feelings.

Phyllis was a strong believer in Mrs. Batts' religion, and in speaking of the above incident, she said:

"I neber seed Satan run outen a meetin' as quick in my born days. 'Rectly old Miss sot down on Mr. Edwards, de devil he tuk out under de flo' and Mr. Edwards hollered 'glory, glory, lemme up," and he got so full ob glory, he thinks ter hissef he gwinter git up anyhow, so he drawed his hind legs up, sorter lak er cow, an' he got up, but not ontwell old Miss had done mashed de devil clean outen him. Mr. Edwards sho' did sweat lak er hoss, but he come up from dat flo' wid mighty good 'ligion."

In writing the Bell Witch story, at times I have seemed to digress, and by way of explanation I would say to the reader, a dark picture needs high lights; and when the esteemed letter carrier on Adams

Route 1, incidentally mentioned the amusing story as given above I could not resist using it, as a high light, believing with Pope: "That a little nonsense now and then, is relished by the best of men."

Several weeks had passed since Betsy Bell had shown signs of a fainting spell; in fact, she had not suffered any special torture from the witch for two months. But there was no hope, seemingly no escape for poor Mr. Bell. He had exhausted every means to free himself and family from the dominion of a mystery that had become a calamity.

Dr. Mize, a noted magician of Simpson county, Ky., came thirty-five miles and spent a week trying to solve the mystery, but his visit, like several others before him, availed nothing.

James Williams Bell, among the best educated of the seven Bell brothers, made intelligent record of the Witch during its three years' torture of his father's family and twenty-eight years later (during the fall and winter of 1846) used the original notes, as a basis for a more comprehensive sketch. From the latter we quote as follows:

"Courageous men in battle line, may rush upon bristling bayonets and blazing musketry, for they can see the enemy, and know who, and what they are fighting, but when it comes to meeting an unknown enemy of demonstrative power, with gall upon its tongue, and venom in its bosom, breathing threats of dire consequences, not knowing in what shape or form the calamity is to come, the stoutest heart will falter. After three years' torture, father gradually declined. Mother and Brother John nursed him with tender care.

"The crisis came on the morning of December 19, 1820. It had been father's custom since he first married to rise early, and wake the Negroes and get the day's work under headway; as a large family of children grew up around him, he continued the habit of arousing the family, the boys seldom awaking till their father's early morning call.

"On the date above mentioned, he failed to call, and upon investigation it was found that he was sleeping soundly, and his breathing was unnatural. Soon he lapsed into a deep stupor and could not be aroused to sensibility. Brother John had given him every dose of medicine he had taken during his last illness, and was very careful that the bottles were labeled and the doctor's directions strictly obeyed.

"Fearing some serious mistake on his part had been made, he examined each bottle in the cupboard, and among them he found a smoky looking vial about one-third full of a dark fluid. The presence of the vial could not be accounted for by any member of the family. Dr. George Hopson, of Port Royal, was sent for in haste, and the near neighbors were called

"In the meantime, Kate broke out in a voice of exultation, 'It's useless for you to try to relieve old Jack Bell, for I've got him this time.' She was then asked about the strange vial of medicine found in the cupboard, and replied: 'I put it there and gave old Jack a big dose of it last night, and it fixed him.'

"On his arrival, Dr. Hopson assured the family he had never seen the vial, and suggested that its contents be tested on something. Brother John ran a straw into the vial and drew it across a cat's tongue. The cat jumped, whirled a few times and expired.

"Dr. Hopson said he detected an odor on father's breath similar to that of the contents of the vial, and when it was thrown into the fire a blue blaze instantly shot up the chimney like a flash of powder.

"Father lay in a stupor twenty-four hours, never regaining consciousness, and on the morning of December 20, 1820, he breathed his last.

"As the grief-stricken family and friends stood around the lifeless body, the question arose, why should such a fate befall a man like John Bell? No mortal man had ever found cause to bring a charge of dishonor to his door, not even the ghostly fiend that haunted him to his death, ever uttered a word that reflected on his honor.

"A great crowd of sorrowing friends attended the funeral. Religious services were conducted by Revs. Sugg Fort, James and Thomas Gunn.

"After the grave was filled and the people turned to leave the graveyard, Kate broke out in a loud voice, singing, 'Row me up some Brandy O,' and continued singing the same line over and over, for several minutes."

The mysterious death of John Bell hung like a pall over the family, in fact, it cast a gloom over the entire community. All eyes and thoughts were now centered on the beautiful young daughter, Betsy, curiously wondering and discussing the probable effect the father's death would have upon her, and the future attitude of the Witch toward her.

Days and weeks passed and the Bell home was seldom without comforting friends. Principal among them was Joshua Gardner.

Betsy was conscious that her heart beat in tender unison with his, and his manly devotion was freely bestowed upon her. But what would be the consequences if she disregarded the warnings of her wicked tormentor? Might not this unseen terror execute its threats on her, as it had already done concerning her father? Could she afford to run the risk of destroying the future happiness of both herself and her lover by yielding to his entreaty to become his wife?

Such was her reasoning in the struggle between love and fear. Kate had ceased meddling in the affairs since Mr. Bell's death, never calling Joshua Gardner's name to Betsy, nor even speaking in his presence. This was encouraging to both, and young Gardner considered it good evidence that the great trouble was nearing the end, and pressed his suit by urging that the marriage should take place at an early date, whereby they could bid good-bye forever to the haunted vale, and go to their long desired home in West Tennessee, near what is now known as Gardner's Station, a few miles distant from Dresden, Tenn.

Pretty Betsy Bell was disposed to yield to his persuasion, by giving her consent conditionally by insisting that their union be postponed a while, awaiting the future course of the Witch.

Kate had seemingly ceased to exist. The rosy flush had returned to Betsy's cheeks, and a bright lustre shone in her pretty blue eyes. "The Fairy Queen of the Haunted Dale" was herself again! The Bell home had resumed something of its former gaiety and a brilliant wedding, long anticipated, was thought to be near at hand.

CHAPTER VIII.

Easter Sunday, April, 1821, found a congenial party of young people at the Bell home, planning for a fishing party to be given by the neighborhood the following day, or what was at that date termed Easter Monday.

The pioneers of Tennessee were inclined to keep alive the Puritan custom of reverently observing the Sabbath and instead of making it a gala day, they celebrated the resurrection on Easter Monday, even the servants on this day being exempt from duty.

Pretty Betsy Bell had at last acceded to Joshua Gardner's pleading and Sunday morning found a beautiful engagement ring on her finger.

Monday morning, bright and early, three happy young couples were wending their way across the Bell meadows on their way to the fishing picnic at Brown's ford on Red river. The couples were Theny Thorn and Alex Gooch, Rebecca Porter and James Long, Betsy Bell and Joshua Gardner. Six happier young people never started out on an Easter outing than the above.

On reaching the beautiful Red river valley, at what was called "The Enchanted Spring," they found a gay crowd of picknickers had already assembled, many of whom had cast their hooks and lines and caught a few fish.

Very soon Prof. Richard Powell, the bachelor school teacher, put in his appearance. He was just out from Springfield on his first canvassing trip as candidate to represent Robertson county in the legislature. He had heard of the fishing party and said he could not resist the temptation to call by and mingle a short while with the group of fine young people who had grown up under his tutelage. He remained an hour or two, and during the time in an undertone said privately to Betsy Bell:

"I have recently learned that you and Josh are about to make a match, and take this occasion to say I wish you happiness." He had observed that Betsy wore a new ring, and supposing it to be her engagement ring, prompted him to take the liberty of referring to a delicate matter.

"That boy never could help loving you, and I did not blame him, although I had, from your earliest girlhood, hoped you might forget that sweet old school day love and that I could possibly become an interested party. Since disappointment is now my seeming fate, I shall at least hope to be at your wedding."

"We shall certainly send you an invitation, Professor," replied Betsy in her characteristic modest manner.

While Mr. Powell remained, he was the central figure of the occasion, but soon as he mounted his fine black horse, waved a graceful good-bye and rode off, the crowd separated, mostly in couples, strolling along the river banks, and over the hillsides, Joshua and Betsy, taking their seat on a moss-covered ledge of rock overlooking the spring. Suddenly a terrible splashing of water in the river not far from them attracted their attention, and Mr. Gardner's pole was jerked from its setting and something, seemingly a huge fish, several feet long, carried it up stream out of sight. Almost before they had time to think it returned, dashing foam and spray high in the air, rendering a clear view as to its identity impossible.

"Look out, it's coming back!" shouted Uncle Zeke Gunn, a faithful old colored fisherman. "I sed sump'm gwine ter happen here today. Dat ain't no fish. I knowed good and well dat Witch wan't gwine er let us hab a day in peace, down heah on de ribber 'joy'n outsefs."

It is needless to say the appearance of this unaccountable water mystery, whatever it might be, left the lovers in a reverie of their own thoughts. The suspense was painful, but the consternation still greater, when the familiar voice of Kate was heard, "Please, Betsy Bell, don't marry Joshua Gardner!" The entreaty was repeated three times, after which the voice gradually died away, as if floating down the river.

The color faded from poor Betsy's cheeks as though a dagger had pierced her heart and the Easter Monday celebration held no further enjoyment for her. The fishing paty was at an end and the young folk began leaving for home an hour or two earlier than they had intended.

On the way, through the woods, and across the fields, toward the Bell home, Betsy summoned courage to ask that the engagement be broken, and the ring returned.

Joshua Gardner had not before fully realized the depth of his love for the queenly young woman who stood before him, but now he tried to plead his cause anew, but the force of her reasoning and firm decision convinced him that all hope was vain. He sadly accepted his fate, but begged her to keep the ring. This she declined to do, by telling him that she considered it a seal to a solemn vow which could not be broken as long as the ring was in her possession. She held out her hand, and in the bitterness of a broken heart, he took it from her slender finger, and they separated that afternoon never to meet again. As soon as he could arrange important business matters, he left for West Tennessee and settled in Obion county.

It was a long time before either of them could overcome the shock of that fateful Easter Monday of April, 1821 .

As time passed, the wound was healed and when Betsy Bell was again seen in the social realm, Hon. Richard Powell was her persistent sutor, and was accepted. She was true to her promise of a few months before that he should be present at her wedding.

While he was many years her senior, he was a man of imposing personality, prominent in public affairs, and one of the best beloved citizens of Robertson county. Their congenial married life was comparatively short, about seventeen years. After his death she remained a widow the balance of her life.

In 1875 she left Tennessee and went to live with one of her children in Mississippi, where she died, 1890, at the advanced age of eighty-six years. Many of her descendants are still living in Robertson county, a number of whom have inherited her fine qualities.

In 1849, the Saturday Evening Post published a comprehensive sketch of the Bell Witch, written by a strolling reporter, who made strenuous efforts to connect Mrs. Betsy Bell Powell with the authorship of the Bell Witch Mystery. Mrs. Powell felt outraged by the injustice and employed a lawyer to institute suit for libel, but the paper retracted and the matter was settled without litigation.

The writer has recently received a letter from Miss Sudie Chambers, a popular teacher of Adairville, Ky., and great-granddaughter of Mr. John Bell. In speaking of the Bell Witch mystery, she said:

"You were correct in supposing that the Bell family never wished any publication of the distorted facts concerning 'Our Family Trouble.' In my opinion, the best written account yet given to the world was that by Irvin Cobb, published in McClure's Magazine of March, 1923, and even that was more legend than fact.

"The original manuscript, or diary kept by my grandfather, Richard William Bell, regarding the mystery was never returned to the Bell family. When last heard from, my uncle, Allen Bell, had loaned it to the late M. V. Ingram, of Clarksville, Tenn., who wrote in book form a comprehensive history of the noted Bell Witch."

Our next installment will deal principally with Kate's return after an absence of seven years.

The voices, both of sacred memory and those still with us in the flesh, who have spoken through this series of Bell Witch articles, have been trustworthy and very few of our readers have been skeptical as to what they said. They have seen and heard every investigation end in confusion, leaving the mystery of all mysteries beyond intelligent explanation.

Richard William Bell, son of John Bell, who kept a faithful record of the events, was known to be among the most reliable citizens of Middle Tennessee, and what he wrote, together with what others of equal veracity told, regarding the Bell Witch, gives us a chain of evidence as strong and complete as seems possible to make any kind of testimony.

In the natural course of events the large Bell family, consisting of seven sons and two daughters, married and scattered, leaving only Mrs. Lucy Bell and two sons, William and Joel, at the old homestead.

In his record William wrote: "The Witch took its departure in 1821, after a four year's untold torture of father's family. In bidding us its farewell it stated that it would return in seven years, which it did, and remained two weeks.

"It made the same demonstrations as when it began 1817. As previously stated Mother was a very discreet woman, and advised us to keep the matter of its return a profound secret, not even telling our brothers and sisters who came to visit us. She seemed to think or fear that publicity might possibly prolong its stay.

The late Mrs. James K. Polk of Robertson county, formerly Miss Mirandy Bell, daughter of Joel Bell and granddaughter of Mr. and Mrs. John Bell, told the writer the interesting story of the Witch's return, after an absence of seven years. Mrs. Polk heard the story direct from the lips of her father, Joel Bell, youngest son of Mr. and Mrs. John Bell, and the older generation now living knew him to be a man of the strictest veracity. He told Mrs. Polk the following:

"One Autumn afternoon in 1828, your grandmother, Lucy Bell, and I were seated in the hall at the old homestead, talking over some family matters, when a dense sulphur smoke filled the hallway from floor to ceiling, and as soon as the smoke cleared away, a black ball as large as a water bucket, seemingly composed of black wool, rolled softly across the hall floor and on into the family room to a wide open fireplace and went up the chimney.

"Not a sound was heard. Mother turned ghastly pale, and walked out into the yard, wringing her hands. I followed and consoled her as best I could. We both had the same thoughts as to what it meant, for we had already begun to think of the seven years' promise or threat to return."

It was only to special friends that Mrs. Polk ever discussed the "Family Trouble," and gave as a reason in her later years that she wanted her children and grandchildren to hear as little of it as possible, lest the unsolved mystery might have a tendency to create unpleasant reflections as to their Bell ancestry.

There was danger of such and she was right in trying to suppress it, knowing as she did that facts had been so distorted. The impress of her forceful character is seen today in her descendants, extending to the fourth generation.

John Wesley, the great founder of Methodism, boasted of his belief in witchcraft. He wrote and spoke prominently about the noted Epworth ghost that haunted the family thirty years. The mysterious and supernatural noises heard in the Epworth rectory were beyond dispute. He said witchcraft and apparitian had been confirmed by reliable testimony of all ages.

Witchcraft troubles began in New England, principally in Massachusetts, in 1645, and by some historians was thought to have reflected on the intelligence of our patriotic forefathers. In 1648, three years later, the charge was brought against Margaret Jones, a young lady of Charlestown, Mass., and she was executed. Ann Hibbons, of Boston, came next, and she was executed in 1656. Here, history says, the subject rested when it was again revived and there was one more execution in Boston.

In 1692 witchcraft broke out in greater fury at Salem and Danvers, Mass. Its first victims were children. At first it affected only the lower classes, but later pervaded all ranks and conditions. Two daughters of a minister in Salem were strangely affected. Before this they had been quiet, happy children, but suddenly began to look wild, shriek, tell strange stories, sit barefoot in the ashes or go abroad with their clothes and hair in great disorder, looking like insane people.

Sometimes they complained of being pricked with pins and were often stricken dumb.

The madness, or whatever it was, spread like a contagion. A devout minister of the gospel was charged with witchcraft, and his former followers turned against him and accused him of having intercourse with the devil. He would not confess guilt and was hanged.

It was a fearful time in our country's history, not knowing when, or where, the disease, or delusion, or whatever it was, would suddenly seize the people. It was not known to any great extent outside of Massachusetts, although an old woman in Pennsylvania, was accused of the crime. The great William Penn happened to be the judge who gave the charge to the jury, which brought in a verdict that her friends should be bound for her to keep the peace, which put an end to witchcraft in that province.

About the time of the greatest excitement in New England, supposed cases of witchcraft were common for centuries in Europe and thousands were executed in England and other European countries.

Strange to say, instead of being regarded as a deplorable affliction it was considered a crime, punishable by hanging and burning at the stake. But not so, 172 years later, when the same affliction came near our homes in the heart of Tennessee, when members of the highly respected Bell family were the recipients of deep and tender sympathy from sources far and wide.